A Taste of Travel

Pacific Press® Publishing Association
Nampa, Idaho
Oshawa, Ontario, Canada
www.pacificpress.com

NANCY LYON KYTE

A Taste of Travel

Vegetarian Soups and Stews From Around the World

Design by Gerald Lee Monks
Cover design resources from iStockphoto.com / Dreamstime.com
Inside design by Pacific Press® Publishing Association

The author assumes full responsibility for the accuracy of all facts and quotations as cited in this book.

Additional copies of this book are available by calling toll-free
1-800-765-6955 or by visiting http://www.adventistbookcenter.com

Library of Congress Cataloging-in-Publication Data

Kyte, Nancy Lyon, 1954-
A taste of travel : vegetarian soups and stews from around the world / Nancy Lyon Kyte.
pages cm
ISBN 13: 978-0-8163-2871-0 (pbk.) ISBN 10: 0-8163-2871-4 (pbk.)
1. Vegetarian cooking. 2. International cooking. I. Title.
TX837.K98 2012
641.59—dc23

2012023473

12   13   14   15   16 • 5   4   3   2   1

Dedicated to Bob,
my husband, best friend,
and trustworthy soup critic.
I thank him with my whole heart.

Acknowledgments

I am so grateful to my sisters, Mary Hellman, Susan Rasmussen, and Sandra Child. From the moment I asked their opinion about whether I should embark on such a project, they urged me to begin right away. Without them, I wouldn't have written even one page. My mother, Marjorie Lyon, loved cookbooks and would have been so proud if she were still living.

In addition, my sisters-in-law, Beverly Jeider, Barbara Kyte, Heather Roeske, and Bobbie Fleck, have been terrific. They helped to keep me focused on getting the job done.

My dad, Mel Lyon, and his wife, Phyllis, have been interested from the beginning. The first soup they tested was the Sweet Potato–Parsnip Soup from New Zealand. Phyllis suggested adding more parsnips, which I did.

I have many people to thank for testing soups. Two of the first people who agreed to critique them are Heidi Moncrief and Nicole Wallace. Others include George and Francis Olsey. Francis was my advisor in the early stages of the project. Her advice was invaluable. I also appreciate Glenn and Nancy Sayers, Nathan and Emily Hellman, Charlotte Ishkanian, and Laurie Falvo for sampling and sharing their opinions. The gentlemen who added insulation to our attic, the folks who came to estimate moving costs, the Aveda staff in Boise, and a crew from Pacific Press® were also willing to share their opinions. These are just a few, and I appreciate each one of them.

Others who have helped me keep going are Julie and Greg Keener, Larry Jeider, Angela Oetman, Gerald and Nadia Oetman, Benjamin Child, and Briana Rasmussen Walker. Bob and Ellen Nixon introduced me to the wonders of fresh herbs, grown in their backyard. I thank Dale Galusha, and many others at Pacific Press® for publishing this book. Sandra Bowman and Beverly Logan have been an encouragement throughout the process. Jerry Thomas, Doug Church, and Bonnie Tyson-Flyn have been supurb.

I also wish to thank Gary and Bettina Krause and my friends at Adventist Mission. Their dedication to their work is a constant inspiration to me personally and professionally. Hans

Acknowledgments

Olson, Rick Kajiwa, Dan Weber, and Charlotte Ishkanian have taken many of the photographs in this book, courtesy of Adventist Mission.

I am grateful to the many hosts and hostesses who have shared hospitality and friendship with me. They have demonstrated that human beings have a great capacity for happy fellowship, honest acceptance, and deep respect for others. I thank them for their warm example.

Last, I want to acknowledge my husband, Bob. Even though I have dedicated the book to him, I must mention that he also tried all of the soups that *didn't* make the book!

Contents

Soups by Country

Contents

Contents

Contents

Contents

Contents

Contents

Some of the fondest memories of my childhood go back to Sabbath mornings. As a Seventh-day Adventist family, we attended church every Saturday. I enjoyed everything about Sabbath School, but what I loved most were the mission stories. I learned that we have a responsibility to care about others and help them in whatever way we can.

Eventually, along with my parents, Melvin and Marjorie Lyon, and my younger sisters, Mary, Susan, Sandra, we became a missionary family. When I was nine years old, we left our home in Des Moines, Iowa, and moved to Bandung, Indonesia. When I was eleven, we were transferred to Japan; and when I was thirteen, we moved to Singapore. Living abroad was a great experience for all of us. I returned to the United States when I was eighteen years old to attend college.

Eventually, I became a Sabbath School teacher in my local church. I enjoyed teaching children about the importance of caring for other people, even folks they didn't know, no matter where they lived in the world. I also believe that it is important that everyone have an opportunity to know God and choose how they will live.

Many years later, I landed the perfect job. As a marketing director for Adventist Mission, I work to raise awareness of the ongoing work that the Seventh-day Adventist Church does in nearly two hundred countries and territories. It is my privilege to share news of upcoming mission projects and report on the work that has been accomplished. I also work to keep our donors updated about the frontline work of Global Mission.

If you are interested in reading current stories, news, and blogs about missionaries and the work they do, you will enjoy visiting the Web site www.AdventistMission.org.

The world is an interesting place, filled with fascinating people living in a variety of cultures. I encourage you to expand your horizons through travel and meeting folks from other countries. Your life will be enriched by your new friends.

With All Due Respect

At no time do I intend to generalize an entire population of one country as being one and the same. Recognizing that individuals are unique, I have looked for commonalities based on research and personal observation. Any misrepresentation is completely unintended.

About the Recipes

The recipes in this book may or may not adequately represent the countries with which they are associated. The recipes are as authentic as possible, based on the availability of the ingredients in North American grocery stores. Some recipes have been chosen or adapted because the primary ingredient of the soup is a leading staple or is readily available in the selected country.

Tips on Utensils and Equipment

You don't need a lot of equipment, but I have found the following basic items useful:

Pans
You should have at least two large pans or stockpots for cooking soup. One should be a heavy pan with a base that will distribute heat evenly for soups that need to simmer for a long time. A large pan with a nonstick coating is also useful.

Spoons
I like to use wooden spoons, both the flat-edged type and the typical curved style. The flat-edged spoons keep food from sticking to the bottom of the pan without scratching the surface.

Measuring Cups
Measuring cups are really useful, but making soup isn't like baking a cake. You don't need to be quite so exact with the measurements. If you have more or less of one ingredient, it's not going to make a big difference. Soup recipes are generally quite forgiving and can tolerate adjustments and substitutions a little better than can other categories of cooking.

Measuring Spoons
Be sure to measure spices and seasonings and take care not to overspice your soup. You can always add more seasoning, but you can't remove it once it's been stirred in. The recipes in this book are middle-of-the-road on the spice scale. If you feel nervous about a new spice, use less. Always adjust seasonings to your personal taste.

Whisk
A good whisk will come in handy when you want to incorporate flour or cornstarch with liquids or to evenly distribute tomato paste in the soup. Besides, who doesn't love to whisk? One whisk should have a nonstick coating to protect your nonstick pans.

Potato Masher
Potato mashers are handy when you want to break up the cooked ingredients for a thicker soup or a consistency somewhere between chunky and smooth.

Tips on Utensils and Equipment

Garlic Press
You don't have to have a garlic press, but it is faster than chopping or mincing garlic with a knife. Once you own a garlic press, you'll never want to be without it.

Cutting Board
Have at least two dishwasher-safe cutting boards on hand. I've had glass ones for years, and I have the dull knives to prove it! Get a couple of good plastic ones. Glass cutting boards are hard on knives and start to dull them right away. Chopping on a plastic cutting board will keep your knives sharper.

Food Chopper
You can always use a knife, but a food chopper will save you time. It also allows you to control the level of coarseness you desire. You might want to use the slicing or grating disc, or the chopping blade of a food processor for some preparations.

Food Processer or Blender
When it comes to making a smooth soup, I prefer a good blender over a food processer. I can usually puree soup in larger batches in a blender. Either one will do the job, but make sure you have a good quality machine that will give you the results you want. Some models have weak motors that tend to burn out.

Hand-held Immersion Blender
If you have an immersion blender, by all means, use it. I've never had one, so I don't miss it. It's a matter of personal preference.

With this equipment on hand, you are ready to get started!

Stock, Broth, and Bouillon

In a very basic sense, stock or broth is the liquid that remains from cooking vegetables. Bouillon cubes are condensed cubes made from the cooking liquid. The cubes are added to cooking water for flavoring. For simplicity, I have used the term "vegetable stock" throughout the cookbook, but you can use stock, broth, or bouillion cubes. Organic, low-sodium, and salt-free varieties are available. You can also make your own stock from the cooking water of vegetables, but potato water is not recommended. It will be starchy and have a cloudy appearance.

Beans

If you are using dried beans, make sure to wash them well and soak them overnight or for at least eight hours. Once they have been soaked, drain them and rinse them again. Be sure to pick out the beans that did not plump up during the soaking period. They will likely stay hard and probably won't cook properly. They aren't worth saving, so just throw them out.

Most of the time one type of bean can be substituted for another kind of bean. If you need white beans but you have only kidney beans, just make the change.

The beans you cook yourself usually taste better, but always keep a good supply of canned beans on hand. Some soups are worth the extra time, but most of the time you need to get the job done quickly. Feel free to adjust and adapt as time permits.

Pepper

I never cook with black pepper, so I haven't included it in any of the recipes in this book. You will find cayenne pepper or chili powder in some recipes, simply because it is typical from that particular region of the world. You can leave it out if you prefer, or you can scale back even further than I already have. Sometimes a hint of spice is all you need. As the cook, you can decide what adjustments you would like to make.

Fresh Herbs Versus Dried Herbs

Fresh herbs such as cilantro, dill, basil, parsley, and mint are wonderful! When you buy fresh herbs, plan to use them so they won't be wasted. The general rule for adjusting fresh herb measurements to dried herb measurements is four to one. In other words, measure four teaspoons of fresh dill in place of one teaspoon of dried dill, and so on. Start easy and make adjustments along the way.

Tomatoes

I love fresh tomatoes, but there are times during the year where good tomatoes are expensive or hard to find. Keep your pantry stocked with canned tomatoes in juice and you can pull together a quick soup at the last minute.

Carrots

I never use frozen carrots because I don't care for the texture, and canned carrots seem too salty. I always use fresh carrots.

Corn, Peas, and Green Beans

I have discovered that recipes that call for corn usually specify either fresh or frozen corn. Canned corn seems to do just as well, so I always keep a few cans on hand.

When it comes to peas, I prefer to use frozen peas. The color is nice and bright, the flavor is good, and the texture is fine. Canned peas tend to be dull in appearance and have a soft consistency. Fresh peas are nice, but they are expensive. Enjoy fresh peas by themselves, or with very little else, so you can get the full benefit of the fresh taste and texture.

Green beans are best when they are fresh and tender, but frozen green beans retain a nice color. Canned green beans are useful and also work well in soups, so it's a good idea to keep a few cans in the pantry.

Squash and Pumpkin

Zucchini and yellow squash taste good and cook quickly. Winter squash and pumpkins are sometimes difficult to cut. When you are short on time, look for butternut squash that has already been peeled and diced. Canned pumpkin will work fine in some soups and stews. Just make sure that the pumpkin doesn't contain all the spices you would expect in pumpkin pie.

Sweet Potatoes and Yams

Sweet potatoes and yams tend to be very solid, dense vegetables, which makes them difficult to cut. Try slicing them into rounds rather than lengthwise. You'll find it much easier to cut through the sweet potato or yam, and then you can dice it quickly.

Onions

It's easy to fall into a pattern of using the same kind of onion for everything. Try the white, red, and yellow varieties. I like sweet onions, but leeks are even sweeter. Green onions are good as last minute additions after the soup is cooked. Scallions are nice too. Try them all for the sake of variety.

Ginger

When using fresh ginger, always remove the peelings before grating or mincing. Throw out any dry knobs. A plump, firm piece of ginger will have the best taste.

Be Bold!

Never be afraid to make changes or adapt recipes according to your own taste. Feel free to try herbs and spices in ways you haven't considered before. Make notes beside the recipes so you can achieve even better results next time.

High Blood Pressure

Using vegetable stock rather than vegetable broth will include flavor without the extra salt.

Try cutting the salt in a recipe in half to reduce sodium and improve the impact on your blood pressure.

Other great ways to improve your blood pressure include reducing or eliminating caffeine and doing regular exercise. Did you know that a daily walk helps your blood pressure in multiple ways? It will improve your cardiovascular fitness, help you reach a healthy weight, and reduce your stress and anxiety.

Diabetes

Did you know that starch from grains, and even some vegetables, can raise your blood sugars? A great way to help minimize the impact on your blood sugars is to choose grains and vegetables that are high in fiber.

When a recipe calls for noodles, opt for a whole-grain noodle, which is high in fiber. When a recipe calls for rice, try a whole-grain version, such as brown rice or wild rice. Be sure to allow for extra cooking time when you use these healthy whole grains.

When preparing a recipe with potatoes, try leaving the skin on for added fiber. Soups with beans are a great source of protein and fiber, both of which can help to keep blood sugars in a healthy range.

Other ways to improve your blood sugars include avoiding beverages such as soda and sports drinks that are high in sugar. It also helps to exercise regularly.

High Cholesterol

Did you know that our bodies make cholesterol from the saturated fat and trans fats that we eat? In a vegetarian diet, saturated fats are most commonly found in dairy products. When a recipe calls for milk, choosing skim milk is a great option that contains no cholesterol-raising saturated fat. Even if you normally drink 2 percent milk or whole milk, chances are you won't notice a difference when you use skim milk in cooking. If a recipe calls for sour cream, try using a light version or a light plain yogurt.

Did you know that foods high in fiber can help lower your cholesterol level? Try choosing whole-grain pastas and whole-grain rice in your soups. Also consider adding a side salad to your soup or stew. Fruits and vegetables are great sources of fiber.

Regular exercise can help to reduce your LDL, or bad cholesterol, and also help to raise your HDL, or good cholesterol.

Regular Checkups

To manage your health and maintain a healthy diet, it is always wise to see your doctor regularly.

Briana Rasmussen Walker, RD, CD
Yakima, Washington

Carrot and Orange Soup

In Afghanistan, oranges are commonly used as a seasoning at the dinner table by squeezing the juice over various dishes. Malta oranges are grown in the warm climate of Nangarhar Province.

INGREDIENTS SERVES 4–6

4 c.	carrots, sliced
2 T.	olive oil
2 cloves	garlic
2 T.	sugar
½ t.	ginger
Just a few	saffron strands
1 c.	orange juice, freshly squeezed
4 c.	water
	salt to taste

GARNISH

Parsley or scalded and dried thin ribbons of orange peel.

PREPARATION

1. Combine the carrots, olive oil, whole garlic cloves, sugar, ginger, and saffron strands in a heavy pan.
2. Cover and cook gently on low heat for 5 to 6 minutes.
3. Add the orange juice and water, and bring to a boil.
4. Turn down the heat and simmer gently for 45 minutes, or until carrots are very tender.
5. Puree in a blender until smooth.

IF YOU GO TO AFGHANISTAN

Hospitality is an essential aspect of Afghan culture. No matter who you are, you will be given the best a family has if you have the opportunity to visit their home. If you are invited for tea, your tea glass will be repeatedly filled. When you have had enough, simply cover the glass with your hand and say *"Bus,"* meaning "enough."

White Bean and Mint Soup

For many years, it was against the law for Albanians to entertain foreigners in their homes, but now they are eager to meet strangers and extend the old traditions of hospitality.

INGREDIENTS SERVES 4–6

2 c.	dry white beans
1	medium onion, chopped
¼ c.	olive oil
4 T.	tomato sauce
2 T.	chopped parsley
½ t.	chili powder
2 T.	mint, chopped
	salt to taste

PREPARATION

1. Wash and soak the beans overnight.
2. Drain and rinse beans.
3. In a large pot, sauté the onion in olive oil until tender.
4. Add the tomato sauce, parsley, and chili powder.
5. Cook for 10 minutes or until a thick sauce forms.
6. Add the beans. Cover the beans with about an inch of water.
7. Add the chopped mint, cover with a lid, and cook for 2 to 3 hours over low heat. (Or use a Crock-Pot and cook on low all day.)
8. Serve hot.

IF YOU GO TO ALBANIA

When entering a traditional home, you will need to remove your shoes. Upon arrival, the host might offer you a pair of slippers or plastic sandals. Do not sit down until you are directed to a chair or cushion of the host's choosing. It is important to know that a nod of the head means No, and a shake of the head means Yes. Placing the palm of your left hand on your chest shows appreciation.

ALGERIA

Spicy Vegetable-Noodle Soup

The country of Algeria lies between Morocco and Tunisia on the southern coastline of the Mediterranean Sea. Sharing a meal is an important part of the culture of hospitality and honor.

INGREDIENTS `SERVES 8–10`

¼ c.	margarine or oil
1	large onion, finely chopped
2 t.	coriander
¼ t.	cayenne pepper
¼ t.	cinnamon
½ t.	salt
2	large tomatoes, diced or 2 cups canned
6 c.	water
1	large potato, peeled and diced
2	medium carrots, peeled and sliced thin
1	medium yellow summer squash, unpeeled (if skin is unblemished), diced
2	stalks celery, diced
1	15-oz. can garbanzos, white beans, or red beans, drained
1 c.	vermicelli (thin spaghetti)

GARNISH

1 medium lemon

PREPARATION

1. In a large, heavy pan, melt the margarine or heat the oil. Stir the onion, coriander, cayenne pepper, cinnamon, and salt until the onions are evenly coated with the spices and herbs. Add the tomatoes and stir well.
2. Add the water and bring to a boil. Add the potatoes, carrots, yellow squash, and celery. Reduce heat and simmer until vegetables are nearly tender.
3. Add the garbanzos, or beans and vermicelli. Add more water if needed.
4. When the noodles are soft, the soup is ready to serve.
5. Ladle into bowls and garnish with a paper-thin slice of lemon.

IF YOU GO TO ALGERIA

Make a point of observing Algerians as they greet each other. There will be handshakes and lengthy questions about family, work, the house, and the weather. They may continue to hold hands after the handshake, or they may hold each other by the arms. When you are dining together, it is helpful to know that some foods may be eaten with your hands. Couscous is eaten with a tablespoon, while stew is eaten with a fork. If you are unsure, follow the example of the folks around you.

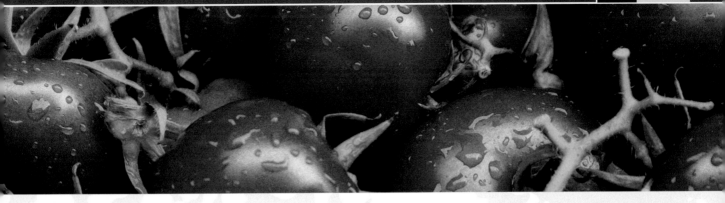

Quick Tomato-Bread Soup

Andorra is a small country tucked between Spain and France, home to the Pyrenees Mountains. This delightfully simple soup is full of flavor, yet delicate in texture. Use fresh tomatoes in the summer, but keep canned tomatoes on hand for a quick and easy supper any time of the year.

INGREDIENTS `SERVES 4–6`

2 or 3 T.	olive oil
1	medium onion, diced fine
3 cloves	garlic
4 c.	tomatoes, peeled and chopped, fresh or canned
3 c.	water
¼ t.	salt
½ loaf	bread (Italian, French, sourdough, or other), cubed
½ c.	fresh basil, loosely packed, chopped

PREPARATION

1. In a large pan, heat the oil and sauté the onion and garlic until the onion is translucent. Do not let them get brown.

2. Stir in the tomatoes, water, and salt. Bring to a boil, then reduce heat and simmer for 15 to 20 minutes.

3. Stir in the bread and basil, taking care not to break up the bread. Cover and allow the bread to absorb the liquid as it heats through. The bread will become puffy. Add more water if the soup seems too thick.

4. Serve hot.

IF YOU GO TO ANDORRA

The tiny country of Andorra is prosperous primarily because of tourism. Skiing in the Pyrenees Mountains is said to be first rate. Hiking trails for every skill level make it possible to enjoy scenic views of mountains, lakes, and valleys. Hot springs are popular with locals and tourists alike. Andorrans are generally a healthy and active group of people. Their life expectancy of 82 years is among the highest in the world. Folk dancing is a charming tradition in this country.

ANTIGUA AND BARBUDA

Pigeon Pea Soup

Pigeon peas are sometimes hard to find, but you might be able to locate them in the international section of your grocery store, the dried bean section, or canned bean aisle. If you can't find them, use any other bean that you like.

INGREDIENTS **SERVES 6–8**

1 T.	oil
1	large onion, chopped
1	large green bell pepper, chopped
4 c.	pigeon peas, cooked and drained (or substitute another kind of bean)
4 c.	vegetable stock
2 c.	water
2 c.	calabaza squash (or substitute Hubbard or butternut squash), diced into 1-inch pieces
1 t.	salt

PREPARATION

1. Heat the oil. Sauté the onion and bell pepper over medium heat for 10 minutes.

2. Add the pigeon peas, vegetable stock, water, squash, and salt. Cover and simmer for 20 to 30 minutes until the squash begins to fall apart. This will thicken the soup.

3. Serve the soup as is, or mash with a potato masher to give the soup a thicker consistency.

IF YOU GO TO ANTIGUA AND BARBUDA

A visit to Antigua and Barbuda would not be complete without visiting the pink sand beaches on the north side of Barbuda. While there, check out the frigate bird rookery in Codrington Lagoon. Listen to the joyful music of steel drum bands; then pick up a CD so you can relive your vacation once you get back home. If you snorkel, take a look at the coral and fish surrounding the shipwreck of the *Andes*.

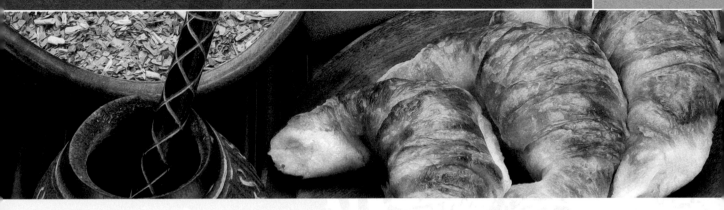

Deluxe Hearts of Palm Soup

The mild-tasting hearts of palm vegetable is harvested from the inner core of certain types of palm trees. Hearts of palm is usually served in salads, but it also transforms this ordinary soup into a gourmet treat. Serve this in your best soup bowls and feel extravagant. *This recipe is in honor of Ricardo and Florencia Bentancur.*

INGREDIENTS `SERVES 4–6`

2 T.	olive oil
1	medium onion, chopped
3	stalks celery, diced
1½ t.	dried basil
2	14-oz. jars hearts of palm, drained and chopped, divided
4 c.	vegetable stock
1½ c.	half-and-half
	salt to taste

GARNISH

1 avocado, peeled and diced

PREPARATION

1. Cook the onions, celery, and basil in olive oil in a heavy saucepan for 4 minutes or until the onion is tender.
2. Reserve ½ c. of the chopped hearts of palm and set aside.
3. Add the remaining hearts of palm and the vegetable stock to the saucepan. Cover and simmer for 25 to 30 minutes. Remove from heat and allow to cool slightly.
4. Puree mixture in a blender.
5. Stir in the half-and-half and reserved hearts of palm. Serve chilled or warm.
6. Garnish with the diced avocado.

IF YOU GO TO ARGENTINA

If you are invited to an Argentine home, be sure to dress well. Arrive 30 to 45 minutes later than the invitation specifies, because arriving on time is not expected. It is appropriate to present your hosts with a gift, but do not give a knife or a pair of scissors. This would indicate that you wish to sever the relationship, and you would miss out on the wonderful Argentine hospitality and excellent cuisine. The widest street in the world is Avenida 9 de Julio, a main thoroughfare in Buenos Aires. It is named after the Argentine Independence Day, which is July 9, 1816. With six lanes of traffic in each direction, it takes several minutes, or about two or three green traffic lights, to cross the avenue at normal walking speed.

ARMENIA

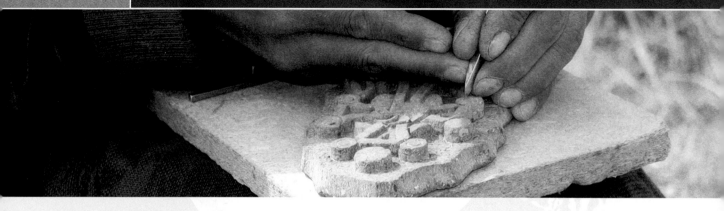

Burnished Apricot–Lentil Soup

In the rural areas of Armenia, don't be surprised or uneasy if a local resident invites you in for tea. The Armenian culture loves to offer hospitality to anyone, even if there is a language barrier.

INGREDIENTS **SERVES 8–10**

3 T.	oil
2	medium onions, diced
4	medium carrots, peeled and chopped
1 T.	cumin
1 t.	coriander
3 c.	red lentils, rinsed
8 c.	water
1¾ c.	dried apricots, chopped, soaked in 1¾ c. of water
	salt to taste

PREPARATION

1. Heat the oil. Sauté the onions and carrots in a heavy pan over medium heat for 10 minutes.
2. Add the cumin and coriander and stir well. Decrease heat to low and cook for an additional 8 to 10 minutes.
3. Add the lentils and enough water to cover. Bring to a boil; then reduce the heat to low and cook for 20 to 25 minutes or until the lentils and carrots are tender. Add water as needed as the lentils soften and swell.
4. Remove from heat and stir in the apricots and the water they soaked in. Add additional water if needed for desired consistency.

IF YOU GO TO ARMENIA

The most common greeting between men is a handshake. If they know each other well, it will be followed by a kiss on the cheek. Women usually greet each other with a hug and a kiss on the cheek, even if they have just met. Between men and women, especially in rural areas, a woman will wait for the man to extend his hand first. Learning to say *jan* (pronounced "john") is a friendly way to address people. For example, Bill *jan* or Megan *jan*. Armenians are friendly people and appreciate it when visitors make an effort to add the term *jan* to their names. For centuries, Armenians have taken rug making to its highest art form, and their handiwork is still in great demand.

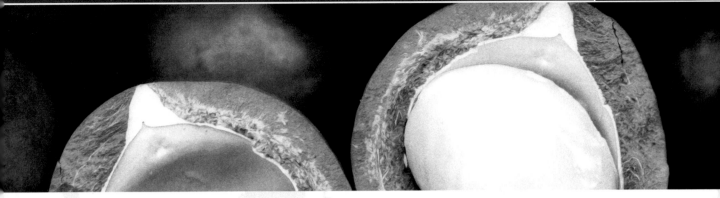

Pumpkin-Macadamia Soup

Long before Australia was mapped by early explorers, it was believed that the aboriginal people enjoyed the seed of a tree they called *gyndl*. Today, it is known as the macadamia nut. These crunchy gems add a bit of taste and luxury to this nutritious pumpkin soup. *This recipe is in honor of Bethany Krause.*

INGREDIENTS `SERVES 4–6`

2 T.	oil
½ c.	macadamia nuts, chopped
1	medium onion, chopped fine
2 t.	fresh ginger, grated
1½ c.	apple, peeled and chopped or grated
3 c.	pumpkin or winter squash, cooked and mashed
3 c.	vegetable stock or water
	salt to taste

GARNISH

Whole or halved macadamia nuts

PREPARATION

1. Heat the oil. Sauté the macadamias, onion, and ginger in a heavy pan for 3 minutes or until golden.
2. Add the apple and stir for 2 minutes.
3. Stir in the pumpkin and vegetable stock.
4. Cover and simmer for 20 to 25 minutes or until apple is soft.
5. May be served as soon as it is cooked, or processed in a blender until smooth and creamy.

IF YOU GO TO AUSTRALIA

You will find that Australians are very open-minded and understanding when it comes to people visiting from other countries. About 27 percent of the population was born to immigrant parents, so there is a general acceptance of a variety of cultures. You will likely be addressed by your first name, even after you have just been introduced. Many world travelers say that Sydney is one of the most beautiful cities in the world, especially its extraordinary harbor. Be sure to enjoy seeing the exotic animals that are native to Australia, and keep an eye out for brightly colored birds you might not see at home.

Paprika-Potato Soup

Simple and satisfying, the familiar flavor of potatoes is enhanced by paprika. If you have all of the ingredients on hand except for the green pepper, use sweet peas as a substitute.

INGREDIENTS SERVES 4–6

1 T.	oil
1	large onion, diced fine
2	medium green bell peppers, chopped
2 T.	flour
4 t.	paprika
6 c.	vegetable stock
5	medium potatoes, peeled and diced
¼ t.	salt

GARNISH

½ c. sour cream or plain yogurt, optional

PREPARATION

1. In a heavy pan, heat the oil and sauté the onion and bell peppers for 8 to10 minutes.

2. Stir in the flour and paprika and mix rapidly to combine. Cook for 2 minutes.
3. Add the stock, potatoes, and salt. Simmer for 20 minutes or until potatoes are tender.
4. Ladle into bowls and top with sour cream, if desired. Sprinkle with additional paprika to add a little color.

IF YOU GO TO AUSTRIA

The family is the most important element of social structure in Austria. Sundays are usually devoted to visiting grandparents or hiking together. Only close friends and family are invited into homes, so invitations to visitors are not common. Etiquette in Austria tends to be formal. People might address each other by their last names rather than their first names. Take in a Mozart concert in Salzburg or listen to waltzes in Vienna if you can.

Yogurt, Walnut, Mint Soup

Choose a thick and creamy plain yogurt, such as Greek-style yogurt, for this delicious recipe. This combination of ingredients results in a pleasant surprise. A fat-free version will not work as well, but a low-fat yogurt version will be fine. Any soup remaining from the meal can be served over baked potatoes the next day.

INGREDIENTS `SERVES 4–6`

2½ c.	plain unsweetened yogurt, thick and creamy (such as Greek style)
2 T.	all-purpose flour
1	large egg
3 c.	water
3 T.	uncooked rice
¾ c.	walnuts, chopped fine
2 cloves	garlic, minced
1½ t.	dried mint, rubbed fine with your fingers
2 T.	olive oil or butter
1	medium onion, chopped fine
1 t.	salt

PREPARATION

1. In a mixing bowl, combine the yogurt and flour and mix well with a whisk or spoon.
2. Add the egg and beat well. Add the water and stir until smooth.
3. Stir in the rice, walnuts, garlic, and mint until combined.
4. In a medium nonstick pan, heat the oil and sauté the onion for about 5 minutes or until tender.
5. Add the yogurt mixture to the pan with the onion. Stir constantly over medium heat for about 20 minutes, or until rice is tender.
6. The cooked soup will be creamy and refreshing. Remove from heat and stir in the salt.
7. Serve hot. Any soup kept for the next day can be served chilled if desired.

IF YOU GO TO AZERBAIJAN

Azerbaijan faces the Caspian Sea and borders Russia and Iran. Baku, the capital city, is a delightful mix of modern and medieval architecture. High in the Caucasus Mountains, you can still see old stone houses untouched by modern times. These homes look as they always have, as if time stood still. It would be nearly impossible to go anywhere without being offered a cup of tea. Even young residents are said to be passionate about offering hospitality to others. The coppersmiths in Lahic are known for their artistic skills. Choose pieces of copperware to take home, and check out hand-knotted rugs.

Papaya Sunset Soup

Papaya is sometimes called "pawpaw." This pretty soup can be served either hot or cold. The pinch of nutmeg adds a subtle flavor.

INGREDIENTS SERVES 4–6

2 T.	butter
1	medium onion, chopped fine
5 c.	papaya, peeled and sliced (slightly firm, not too ripe)
3 c.	water
¾ t.	salt
1 pinch	nutmeg
3 c.	milk
1 T.	cornstarch

GARNISH

If serving this soup cold, garnish with cucumbers, sliced paper thin.

PREPARATION

1. In a large pan, melt the butter and fry the onion until tender.
2. Add the papaya, water, and salt. Cover and cook for 40 minutes, or until the papaya is very soft.
3. Puree in a blender until smooth. Return to the pan.
4. Add the nutmeg. Add the cornstarch to the milk, stirring until smooth. Add to the papaya mixture and reheat. Stir constantly for 10 minutes, but do not let the soup come to a boil.
5. Serve hot, or cool to room temperature, and refrigerate before serving cold.

IF YOU GO TO THE BAHAMAS

There are so many islands in the Bahamas, you could visit a different one every day for more than a year before you would cover them all. If you count the bits of limestone sticking up out of the water, it could take more than five years. One way to island hop is to catch a ride on the mail boat as it makes its rounds. Kayaking is another way to get a good view of some of the stunning beaches. Diving to view remnants of shipwrecks on the ocean floor is a novelty for the adventurous visitor. Bahamians tend to be kind and welcoming, exhibiting good humor and a zest for life. Good manners are appreciated.

BAHRAIN

Tomato-Garbanzo Soup

Here is a nutritious soup that is easy on the budget, especially if you cook the garbanzos yourself. When you're short on time, use the canned variety. If you have all the ingredients except for the garbanzos, just use red beans, baby lima beans, or other beans you have on hand.

INGREDIENTS SERVES 6–8

1 T.	olive oil
1	large onion, chopped
3 cloves	garlic, minced
¼ c.	cilantro leaves, chopped fine
3 c.	garbanzos, cooked
3 c.	tomato juice
5 c.	water
⅓ c.	rice
1 t.	salt
½ t.	allspice
⅛ t.	cayenne pepper, optional

PREPARATION

1. Heat the oil in a large pan, then sauté the onion and garlic over medium heat for 10 minutes.

2. Add the remaining ingredients and bring to a boil. Cover and cook over low heat for 35 minutes or until rice is cooked.

IF YOU GO TO BAHRAIN

Bahrainis are known to be enthusiastic people who delight in hospitality. They entertain at home and in restaurants. The cuisine is excellent, and your plate will likely be replenished several times. It is considered polite to leave a little food on your plate when you are finished eating. This demonstrates that your host has showered you with generous abundance. It would be in very good taste to reciprocate the hospitality if you can. A man should not bring flowers as a gift, but a woman could give them to the hostess. Otherwise, any gift should be given by the man to the host, never to the hostess.

Red Bean and Bell Pepper Soup

Bay leaves and bright colors are always in plentiful supply in the Caribbean Islands. This soup has both, plus a whole lot of taste and nutrition.

INGREDIENTS SERVES 6–8

8 c.	vegetable stock or water
2¼ c.	dried red beans, soaked overnight (or a 1 lb. bag)
1	medium Cubanelle pepper, halved and seeded (or two jalapeño peppers)
2	bay leaves
1 T.	oil
1 each	red, green, yellow, or orange bell pepper, chopped fine
1	large onion, chopped fine
3 cloves	garlic, minced
½ c.	tomato paste
1	medium potato, peeled and diced
2	medium yellow crookneck squash or yellow zucchini, peeled and diced
1 t.	salt
½ c.	cilantro, chopped

PREPARATION

1. Rinse and drain the red beans and place in a large stockpot with the vegetable stock or water.
2. Add the Cubanelle pepper and bay leaves. Bring to a boil, then reduce heat and partially cover the pot. Simmer for 1 hour. Discard the Cubanelle pepper and bay leaves. Remove from heat and set the pot aside.
3. While the beans are simmering, heat the oil in a large skillet. Sauté the bell peppers, onion, and garlic. Cook until the onions are soft.
4. Stir in the tomato paste and mix well. Add the cooked pepper mixture and the potatoes to the beans and cook for 15 minutes.
5. Add the crookneck squash or zucchini and salt. Simmer for about 10 minutes or until all vegetables are tender.
6. Add the cilantro before serving.

IF YOU GO TO BARBADOS

The island is actually more about back roads and old plantations than beaches, but all roads eventually lead to the coastline. A walk on white sand beaches could yield some interesting seashells, but keep a watchful eye out for a message in a bottle. Look for paintings of fishing boats and gardens with a riot of tropical flowers.

Creamy Belgian Endive Soup

Many Belgians remain in the town in which they were raised, a custom that tends to create close extended families. The obligation to one's family is a top priority. This delicious soup is meant to be enjoyed in the company of those you love.

INGREDIENTS SERVES 4–6

2 T.	margarine or butter
2 heads	Belgian endive, sliced thin (discard core)
1	medium white onion, chopped
1 clove	garlic
2	large potatoes, peeled and diced
2 c.	vegetable broth or water
1 c.	milk or fat-free half-and-half
	salt to taste

GARNISH

Chopped chives or dill sprigs

PREPARATION

1. Melt the margarine. Sauté the endives, onion, and garlic for 3 minutes.

2. Add potatoes and vegetable broth or water. Bring to a boil, then reduce heat to low and simmer for about 15 minutes or until potatoes are tender.
3. Place the mixture, in two or three batches, into a blender. Blend until smooth. In each batch, add some of the milk or half-and-half and blend again.
4. Garnish as desired.
5. Serve hot or cold.

IF YOU GO TO BELGIUM

When entering a Belgian home, you should shake hands with everyone present, even the children. Bring flowers (but not white chrysanthemums, which are associated with death) or good quality chocolates for the hostess. You will make a great impression on the family if you bring a small gift, such as candy, for the children. Never leave food on your plate, as this would be considered wasteful. No matter how curious you might be, it would be impolite to ask for a tour of the house.

Easy Green Chile Stew

This soup comes together so quickly, no one will believe you haven't spent a lot of time and effort on it. The green enchilada sauce yields a nicer result than the red enchilada sauce, but you can use either style.

INGREDIENTS `SERVES 8–10`

1	15-oz. can black beans, undrained
1	15-oz. can kidney beans, undrained
1	15-oz. can garbanzo beans, undrained
1	15-oz. can black-eyed peas, undrained
1	28-oz. can diced tomatoes, with juice
1	30-oz. can green chile enchilada sauce
1 c.	pumpkin, canned, unsweetened
1	4-oz. can chile peppers, chopped
1 t.	salt

GARNISH

½ c. sour cream, optional
3 medium avocados, optional

PREPARATION

1. In a large stockpot, combine the beans and the tomatoes and cook over medium heat, stirring frequently until heated through.
2. Stir in the enchilada sauce, pumpkin, chile peppers, and salt. Reduce heat to low and simmer gently until the stew is hot enough to serve.
3. Ladle into bowls and garnish with sour cream and avocado slices if desired.

IF YOU GO TO BELIZE

Mealtimes are communal occasions, meaning that some schools and businesses close for a long lunch break so that families can eat together or rest. The daily schedule resumes later in the afternoon. Belize is the only country in Central America where English is the official language. Spanish and other regional languages are also common. The second largest barrier reef in the world is located in the northern cayes. Snorkeling is said to be fantastic, but you'll also want to keep an eye out for the five-foot-tall Jabiru stork, a common sight in the Crooked Tree Wildlife Sanctuary.

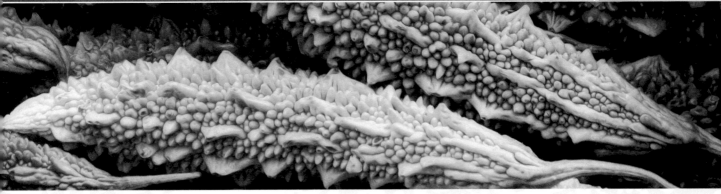

Gluten-Pepper Stew

Due to its geographical location, Bhutanese cuisine has been influenced by China, Tibet, and India. Rice plays an important role in the daily diet in all four countries. This chunky stew is delicious served over steamed rice. If you like hotter peppers than jalapeños, go ahead and turn up the heat with a spicier variety.

INGREDIENTS   SERVES 4–6

1 T.	oil
4 c.	gluten or seitan, chopped or sliced into thin strips
6 cloves	garlic
1	large onion, chopped
2	medium jalapeños, seeded and chopped fine
2 T.	white grape juice or lemonade
1½ c.	tomatoes, fresh or canned, diced
4 c.	vegetable stock
½ t.	salt
2 T.	cilantro, chopped

PREPARATION

1. In a large pan, heat the oil and sauté the gluten or seitan, garlic, onion, and jalapeños until slightly brown.

2. Stir in the juice, tomatoes, salt, and vegetable stock. Cover and simmer for 30 minutes over low heat. Add more stock or water if necessary.

3. Add the cilantro just before serving.

IF YOU GO TO BHUTAN

The people of Bhutan are known for their warmth and friendliness, but while visitors enjoy the privilege of their hospitality, it is important to show respect at all times. Many Bhutanese celebrations have religious significance. The grounds on which the festivals are held are consecrated and are therefore considered sacred. Keep the volume down when you speak— loud voices are offensive. Some lakes are considered sacred, so it is best to avoid washing or swimming in them. Do not throw things into any of the lakes because it could be considered highly irreverent. Observe the local etiquette and act accordingly. Upon meeting people, a nod of the head or a slight bow is appreciated.

Lima Bean–Vegetable Soup

Because all of these ingredients are easy to find, your pantry might already be stocked with them. The marjoram and oregano add something special to the lima beans.

INGREDIENTS **SERVES 6–8**

6 c.	vegetable stock
3 to 4 c.	lima beans, cooked (if using canned, rinse and drain)
3	medium carrots, sliced thin
2	medium potatoes, peeled and diced
1	large sweet red bell pepper, chopped
1	large onion, chopped
2	stalks celery, sliced thin
2 T.	oil
1½ t.	marjoram
¾ t.	oregano
½ t.	salt
1 c.	half-and-half or light cream

PREPARATION

1. In a large, heavy stockpot, combine all ingredients except for the half-and-half or cream.
2. Bring to a boil over medium heat.
3. Reduce heat, cover, and simmer for 25 to 35 minutes, or until the vegetables are tender.
4. Add the half-and-half or cream. Heat, but do not boil.

IF YOU GO TO BOLIVIA

Never eat food with your hands, unless sandwiches. Forks and knives are used at all times. If you are dining with others, you should avoid checking your watch during the meal. Most important, do not put your elbows on the table, even for a moment. This would show great disrespect and could directly affect the relationship you have with your hosts. Your elbows will determine whether you are trustworthy and whether you will be welcomed in the future. Guests are always served first; however, you should not begin to eat or drink until after your host takes the first bite or sip. Meals often last for one or two hours. Because most of the socializing takes place during this time, the general rule is to leave about 30 minutes after the meal, or no later than an hour. When shopping for gifts to take back home, look for items that showcase the colorful art of Bolivian weaving.

BOSNIA AND HERZEGOVINA

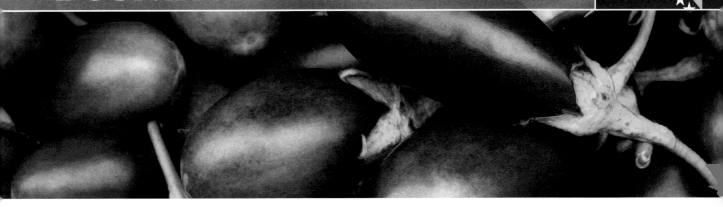

Chilled Eggplant and Buttermilk Soup

This mild-tasting soup might remind you of a Middle Eastern dip for bread. In fact, if you have any soup left over, you can use it as a dip the next day.

INGREDIENTS SERVES 4–6

2	medium eggplants, whole
5 cloves	garlic, unpeeled
3	medium tomatoes, whole
4 T.	olive oil
½ t.	dried oregano leaves
4 c.	lowfat buttermilk
¼ to ½ t.	red pepper flakes, optional
	salt to taste
1 t.	lemon zest

PREPARATION

1. Preheat oven to 400°F. Line a large baking pan with aluminum foil. Place the eggplants, garlic, and tomatoes in the pan. Roast for 40 minutes, turning occasionally. Vegetables should be blistered and blackened on all sides, and tender when pierced with a knife.
2. Remove pan from oven, cover with another sheet of aluminum foil, and allow to steam until the vegetables are cool enough to handle.
3. Squeeze the garlic from its skin and place in a blender. Remove and discard the skins from the eggplants and tomatoes. Add the eggplant and tomato pulp to the blender, including the seeds. Puree until smooth.
4. While the machine is running, slowly add the olive oil, oregano, buttermilk, and red pepper flakes (optional), and salt.
5. Add lemon zest and refrigerate for at least 2 hours.

IF YOU GO TO BOSNIA AND HERZEGOVINA

Most people in Bosnia and Herzegovina prefer to eat at home. For many, eating at a nice restaurant is a rare treat, but they don't mind buying snacks from street vendors or meeting friends for coffee or tea at a local café. The main meal of the day is a late lunch. Leftovers from lunch are eaten in the evening. In general, people tend to stand close together and speak loudly. Staring at someone is not considered impolite, so don't take offense. Folks might be curious about you, or maybe they just like your shirt or hairstyle. Strangers nod to one another in passing. Failure to greet someone when a greeting is expected is considered a serious breach of etiquette.

Pumpkin-Corn Soup

It is widely known that folks in Botswana prize a good pumpkin. One can only imagine how many ways pumpkin can be cooked by the inventive folks who live there, but here is one good example.

INGREDIENTS `SERVES 4–6`

2 T.	margarine
1	large onion, chopped
1	medium sweet red bell pepper, chopped
2 c.	fresh or frozen corn, thawed
2	medium jalapeño peppers, chopped fine
2 cloves	garlic, minced
1 t.	chili powder
4 c.	vegetable stock
1¾ c.	canned pumpkin
½ t.	salt
1 t.	nutmeg
2 T.	fresh lemon or lime juice

PREPARATION

1. In a large pan, heat the margarine and sauté the onion and red pepper for 5 minutes or until almost tender.
2. Add the corn, jalapeños, garlic, and chili powder. Cook for 2 minutes.
3. Stir in the vegetable stock, pumpkin, salt, and nutmeg. Bring to a boil, and then reduce heat. Cover and simmer for 10 minutes.
4. Stir in the lemon or lime juice.

IF YOU GO TO BOTSWANA

Floodplains and wilderness make up the migration corridor for elephants and all manner of wildlife, including thousands of zebras. Lions and wild dogs roam the area and hide in tall grass, tracking their next meals. Strong respect is shown to elders. You would be wise to show your respect as well by deferring to elders, giving up your seat if none are available, or asking for their advice or opinions. When you say hello, be sure to add the appropriate "ma'am" or "sir"; otherwise the greeting will seem incomplete. Always be sure to greet someone before asking for directions, ordering at a restaurant, or making any kind of request.

Black Bean and Sweet Potato Stew

Don't expect to grab a quick lunch in Brazil. Meals are very important in both social and business settings, and they tend to last a long time. Lunch can sometimes last for two hours. With this stew, lovely to look at and delightful to taste, you won't want to rush. *This recipe is in honor of Jabson and Marileide Da Silva.*

INGREDIENTS SERVES 4–6

2 T.	oil
1	onion, chopped
2 cloves	garlic, minced
2	medium sweet potatoes or yams, peeled and diced
1½ c.	water
4 c.	black beans, cooked, or 2 16-oz. cans, drained and rinsed
1	large red bell pepper, chopped
1 c.	diced tomatoes
1	jalapeño pepper, seeds removed, chopped fine
¼ c.	cilantro, chopped
	salt to taste

PREPARATION

1. Heat the oil in a large soup pot. Sauté the onion until clear.
2. Add the garlic and cook until onion is golden.
3. Add the sweet potatoes or yams and water. Bring to a boil, then simmer in the covered pot for 10 to 15 minutes or until the sweet potatoes or yams are tender but still firm.
4. Add the beans, bell pepper, tomatoes, and jalapeño pepper.
5. Simmer on very low heat for 15 minutes.
6. Stir in the cilantro and season with salt to taste.
7. Serve over hot cooked rice.

IF YOU GO TO BRAZIL

Brazilians value fashion, and they will take note of what you are wearing. Be sure to wear clean, stylish shoes. It is usually best not to wear green and yellow together, as these colors are usually reserved for the national flag. In a social setting, arrive a half hour late. Arriving early at someone's home is considered thoughtless because your hosts might not be ready for you. If it is a large event, arrive one hour late. For a business appointment, arrive on time, even though you might be kept waiting.

Fresh Fennel Soup

Fennel is one of those mysterious light-green vegetable bulbs you see in the grocery store, but most people don't seem to know how to use it. It is sometimes called sweet anise, known for its slight licorice taste. In some places, fennel is considered an invasive weed, but in other areas it is prized for its medicinal qualities. Whether you find fennel growing wild along the roadside or recognize it as a popular ingredient with professional chefs, you'll wonder why you waited so long to try it. *This recipe is in honor of Virginia Lee.*

INGREDIENTS SERVES 4–6

1 T.	olive oil
1	medium onion, chopped
2 cloves	garlic, minced
3	medium fennel bulbs, cored and cut into small pieces (discard stalks)
1 c.	feathery tops of the fennel, snipped, divided
2	potatoes, peeled and diced
4 c.	water
½ c.	half-and-half or milk, optional
	salt to taste

GARNISH

2 T. fennel tops

PREPARATION

1. Heat the olive oil in a large saucepan. Sauté the onion for 4 minutes, or until the onion softens.

2. Add the minced garlic and cook for 3 minutes, stirring constantly.
3. Add the pieces of fennel bulb and tops (reserving 2 tablespoons for garnish), potatoes, and water. Bring to a boil; simmer for 20 minutes.
4. Puree the soup in a blender. Add the half-and-half or milk, if using.
5. Ladle soup into bowls; garnish with the fennel tops.

IF YOU GO TO BULGARIA

Bulgaria is a fairly formal society, so it is important to address people by Mr., Mrs., or Ms., followed by their surname. Only friends and family address each other by their first names. On the other hand, dining etiquette is quite informal. It is helpful to know that eating more food shows appreciation, so take small servings to start with. This will allow you to compliment your hosts by accepting second servings. Empty glasses are always refilled; so if you don't want any more to drink, leave a small amount at the bottom of your glass. Bulgarians are proud of their many national parks and beautiful waterfalls. Bulgaria is one of the most visited countries in southeast Europe.

Cool Avocado Soup

With the cool taste of avocados and yogurt, this chilled soup is a welcome prelude to a summer meal.

INGREDIENTS SERVES 4–6

3	medium ripe avocados
4 c.	vegetable stock
2 T.	fresh lime juice
2 T.	plain yogurt
3 or 4 dashes	chili sauce, optional
¼ t.	salt

GARNISH

Yogurt and paprika, optional

PREPARATION

1. Puree the avocados in a blender, gradually adding the vegetable stock.
2. Blend in the lime juice, yogurt, chili sauce, and salt.
3. Refrigerate for at least one hour.
4. Stir before serving.
5. Garnish with additional yogurt and paprika if desired.

IF YOU GO TO BURKINA FASO

Approximately 90 percent of the citizens of Burkina Faso live in about 8,000 villages in rural areas. Extended families help to raise children, work together on small farms, and share cooking responsibilities. If a husband should die, a woman is usually expected to marry one of his brothers. Infants up to two or three years old are in almost constant physical contact with a mother, sister, or aunt. They are tied to their caregiver's back in a wrapper. Firstborn children have great responsibility for younger siblings. When the national flag is being lowered, everyone is expected to stand still until it is properly folded.

BURUNDI

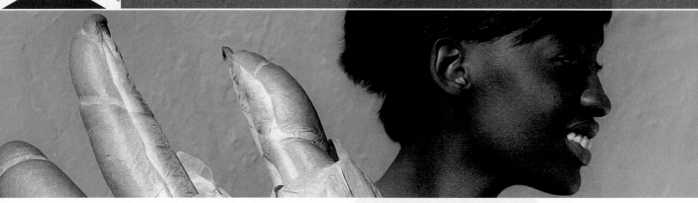

Mixed Bean and Celery Soup

The landlocked country of Burundi has distinctive wet and dry seasons, making it difficult at times to grow enough food to support one's family. In good years, beans are dried and stored, helping the people survive the ravaging famines of bad years.

INGREDIENTS `SERVES 6–8`

2 T.	oil
1	large onion, chopped coarsely
5	stalks celery, sliced thin
2 c.	white lima beans, precooked
2 c.	red beans, precooked
2 c.	white beans, precooked
½ t.	red chili powder
4 c.	tomato juice
1 c.	water
2 T.	fresh basil, chopped
1 t.	salt
¾ c.	peanuts, chopped fine, optional

PREPARATION

1. In a large, heavy pan, heat the oil and sauté the onion and celery until tender.
2. Add the beans, pepper, tomato juice, water, basil, and salt.
3. If the soup seems too thick, add more tomato juice or water.
4. Add the peanuts if you are using them.

IF YOU GO TO BURUNDI

A visit to Lake Tanganyika is a must. It covers more than 12,700 square miles, with a shoreline of more than 1,000 miles. It is the deepest lake in Africa, with an average depth of more than 1,800 feet. The lake holds many species of brightly colored fish, making them very popular in freshwater aquariums. Because drumming is an important part of Burundian cultural heritage, try to take in a performance. The drummers are reported to be magnificent. A tribal drum would make a great souvenir.

Cilantro-Lime Soup

Pretty to look at and lovely to eat, the lime juice and cilantro brighten the flavors of the other vegetables. Gram flour, which has a specific taste, is actually garbanzo flour. It can be found in the international food aisle of most grocery stores, but you can substitute wheat or rice flour instead. *This recipe is in honor of Lim Teng Pheng.*

INGREDIENTS SERVES 4–6

2 T.	oil
1	medium onion, chopped
1	medium leek, white part only, chopped
4 cloves	garlic, minced
1 t.	fresh ginger, grated
2 T.	gram flour
4 c.	vegetable stock
2 c.	chopped cabbage
2	medium carrots, halved lengthwise and sliced thin
3 T.	cilantro, chopped and divided
2 T.	fresh lime or lemon juice
1 T.	soy sauce

PREPARATION

1. Heat the oil in a pan. Add the onion, leek, garlic, and ginger. Fry over medium heat, stirring frequently, until translucent.
2. Stir in the flour and cook for 1 minute.
3. Add the vegetable stock, cabbage, carrots, and half of the cilantro leaves. Bring to a boil and cook for 8 to 10 minutes until the cabbage and carrots are just tender.
4. Stir in the lime or lemon juice, remaining cilantro, and soy sauce. Bring soup to a boil again. Serve immediately.

IF YOU GO TO CAMBODIA

It would be difficult to find another country where the people are as friendly as the Cambodians. They are curious about tourists and enjoy conversations with foreigners. They may ask many questions about your homeland because they are sincerely interested. If you are included in a social situation, wait until you are told where to sit. Seating arrangements tend to follow a pattern of hierarchy, so the oldest person is usually seated first. Always wait until that person has started eating before you take your first bite. Take care that you do not appear boastful or proud; modesty and humility are important virtues here.

Millet-Vegetable Soup

Everyone likes a hearty soup when the weather turns cool. The millet is filling, so this soup could easily be a meal in itself. You can vary the vegetables if you wish, but the base should include onions, celery, and carrots.

INGREDIENTS   SERVES 4–6

2 T.	olive oil
1	medium onion, chopped
2	stalks celery, chopped
4 or 5	carrots, chopped
1	medium turnip or rutabaga, peeled and chopped
2	medium sweet potatoes or yams, peeled and chopped
1	bay leaf
2	thyme stems
4 c.	vegetable stock
2 c.	water
½ t.	salt
1 c.	millet

PREPARATION

1. Heat the olive oil in a large pan and sauté the onion, celery, and carrots for 5 minutes or until tender.

2. Add the turnip or rutabaga, sweet potatoes or yams, bay leaf, thyme, vegetable stock, water, and salt. Bring to a boil, cover, reduce heat, and cook for 15 minutes.

3. While the soup is cooking, toast the millet in a small dry skillet over medium heat for 5 minutes, stirring frequently.

4. Add the millet to the soup and cook for an additional 20 minutes until the millet and vegetables are tender.

5. Remove the bay leaf and thyme stems. (The thyme leaves will fall off the stems and cook into the soup.)

IF YOU GO TO CAMEROON

While visiting Cameroon, refrain from wearing shorts, even if it is hot outside. Men should wear long pants, and women should wear long skirts. It is wise to plan ahead by preparing a small stash of gifts, just in case you need them. Gifts, including cooked and uncooked food, are symbols of kinship and bonding. Fruit, nuts, chocolates, and candies are perfect for such occasions. The sharing of a meal is one of the most valued ways to express hospitality and trust. Depending on the size of the village or small town in rural areas, a market may be open once every week or two, or perhaps daily.

CANADA

Yellow Split-Pea Soup

This traditional French Canadian soup is common at home and in restaurants in Quebec, but is a favorite all across Canada. *Inspired by my sister-in-law, Heather Roeske, the best cook in Canada.*

INGREDIENTS SERVES 6–8

2 T.	oil
1	large onion, chopped fine
3	stalks celery, chopped fine
3	carrots, chopped fine
2 c.	yellow split peas, uncooked
9 c.	water
2	bay leaves
1 t.	thyme
2 T.	chickenlike seasoning
2 t.	smoke-flavored yeast flakes, optional
2	medium potatoes, peeled and grated
	salt to taste

PREPARATION

1. In a large, heavy pan, heat the oil and sauté the onion, celery, and carrots until the onion is clear.

2. Add the split peas, water, bay leaves, thyme, chickenlike seasoning, and yeast flakes. Bring to a boil; then reduce heat and simmer over low heat for about 60 minutes.
3. Add the potatoes and cook for 10 to 15 minutes until the soup thickens, or until the potatoes are tender.
4. Remove the bay leaves.
5. Puree in a blender until smooth. Return to pan and reheat.
6. Add salt if needed.

IF YOU GO TO CANADA

Canada has two national sports, each with loyal and avid fans. Lacrosse, introduced by the First Nations people, is played in the summer, while ice hockey is played in the winter. In the eighteenth century, the Hudson's Bay Company began trading tools, copper kettles, blankets, and trinkets for beaver pelts and other furs. Traditional Hudson's Bay Company blankets are marked with a varying number of short black stripes. The number of stripes indicated the size of the blanket. The most recognizable symbols of Canada are the maple leaf, beaver, and Canada goose.

Spinach-Pepper Stew

Green bell peppers and spinach grow quickly, making them readily available as ingredients for soups and stews in central African countries. When weather and crops are good, families enjoy three meals each day. During hungry times, which sometimes occur before crops are harvested, people may have to cut back to two, or even one meal per day.

INGREDIENTS SERVES 4–6

1½ T.	oil
1	medium onion, chopped fine
2	large tomatoes, peeled and chopped (or 1 15-oz. can of tomatoes with juice)
2	medium green bell peppers, chopped
1 c.	water
2	10-oz. pkg. frozen spinach, thawed and drained
½ t.	salt
⅛ t.	cayenne pepper
¼ c.	peanut butter

PREPARATION

1. In a large stew pot, heat the oil and sauté the onion over medium-high heat until golden.
2. Stir in the tomatoes and green bell pepper. Cook for 3 minutes.
3. Add the water, chopped spinach, salt, and cayenne pepper. Simmer for 5 minutes.
4. In a separate bowl, thin the peanut butter with several tablespoons of the hot liquid. Add the peanut butter mixture to the stew. Continue to simmer for another 10 to 15 minutes, stirring frequently.
5. For a spicier stew, adjust the amount of cayenne pepper, adding a little at a time until it reaches the heat level you like.
6. Serve with rice or a stiff porridge.

IF YOU GO TO THE CENTRAL AFRICAN REPUBLIC

Food can be a precious commodity in the Central African Republic; but when people have it, they are willing to share it. If you are a guest, be humble, don't overeat, and be sure to offer a sincere compliment. Expressing good wishes for the health of the hosts is a polite gesture and greatly appreciated. Do not openly admire an object in someone's home or they might feel obligated to give it to you. Look for ebony wood-carvings or handmade items for souvenirs.

Chilled Strawberry Soup

Strawberries have grown wild in Chile for hundreds of years. Most Chilean strawberries are sold fresh within the domestic market, but the country has a significant export market as well. Fresh fruit soups are often made with a syrup base, but this one requires sugar only if the strawberries or fruit juice are tart. See the variations listed below.

INGREDIENTS SERVES 4–6

4 c.	strawberries, hulled
1½ c.	orange juice
1 T.	lemon juice
2 T.	sugar, if needed

VARIATIONS

Add a dash of cinnamon and a pinch of allspice

PREPARATION

1. Combine all ingredients in a blender, working in batches if necessary, and puree until smooth.
2. Refrigerate until thoroughly chilled.

HOW TO SERVE

- This soup can be sipped from a teacup or small glass.
- Serve in bowls over fresh strawberries or fruit salad.
- Ladle over pound cake.
- Serve with scones, banana bread, or English muffins on the side.

IF YOU GO TO CHILE

One of the beloved traditions in Chile is watching cowboys demonstrate their expertise at the rodeo. The *huasos* are highly skilled and confident, proud of their place in Chilean history. Each spring, the cowboys round up the cattle and corral them for sale and branding. It requires an intense amount of teamwork between the cowboy and his horse. The horses are trained to gallop sideways, which gives them the advantage when moving cattle into a rounded enclosure without roping. For special events, cowboys wear a dress version of their work clothes. At the rodeo, you will likely see cowboys wearing loose fitting pants, usually striped, a short jacket, fringed leather boots, and a colorful blanket or poncho worn thrown over the shoulders. A red sash is worn around the waist with the fringed ends over the left hip. For ceremonial events, the stirrups are elaborately carved in wood or leather. The spurs contain brass or copper ornamentation.

Snow Pea and Bok Choy Soup

Fresh snow peas and tender bok choy are classic ingredients in Chinese cooking. This is a perfect addition to any springtime menu.

INGREDIENTS SERVES 4–6

4 c.	vegetable stock
1 c.	bok choy, chopped fine
½ c.	white mushrooms, sliced thin
1 c.	tofu, cut into small cubes
1 clove	garlic, minced
½ t.	grated fresh ginger
1 c.	fresh snow peas
5	medium green onions, including tender portion of green tops

PREPARATION

1. In a large pan, bring the vegetable stock, bok choy, mushrooms, tofu, garlic, and ginger to a boil. Reduce heat and simmer for 20 minutes.
2. Add the snow peas and green onions. Cook for 5 minutes.
3. Ladle into bowls. The soup may also be served over a scoop of rice.

IF YOU GO TO CHINA

If you don't know how to use chopsticks, ask someone to teach you the basics. While you are learning, there are a few basic guidelines to keep in mind so that you don't appear to be uncultured. The host or hostess will likely have the longest chopsticks so that he or she can reach for food and place it on the guests' plates. Use your chopsticks to reach for food that is closest to you on the communal platter without digging through the food. Since you will likely be eating family style, it is important to keep your lips from touching the food on your chopsticks. Never let your chopsticks stand upright or vertical in your bowl. This is a gesture reserved for honoring deceased family members, so it is not appropriate at the table. When you are not using your chopsticks, place them on the chopstick rest or beside your bowl or plate. Playing with your chopsticks or using them to make drumming sounds will decrease your social status.

Sancocho

Sancocho is traditionally made with chunks of corn on the cob cooked into the soup. When fresh corn isn't available, you can use frozen or canned corn instead. Sazon seasoning can be found in the Hispanic food section of your grocery store. *This recipe was inspired by Isabel Sarria.*

INGREDIENTS SERVES 4–6

6 c.	water
4 c.	vegetable stock
4 c.	corn, frozen or canned (or 3 ears of corn cut into 3-inch pieces)
½ t.	salt
2 or 3	medium green plantains, peeled and cut crosswise into 2-inch pieces
6	medium white potatoes, peeled and quartered
1	medium green bell pepper, diced
2 c.	yuca root, cut into chunks
1 c.	giso (see below)
⅓ c.	cilantro, chopped

INGREDIENTS FOR GISO

1	large tomato
1	small red bell pepper, chopped
5	medium green onions

¼ t.	cumin
½ t.	salt
2 cloves	garlic
½ T.	sazon seasoning (or substitute ¾ t. paprika and ¾ t. coriander)

PREPARATION OF SANCOCHO

1. Place the water, vegetable stock, corn, salt, and plantains in a large pot of water. Bring to a boil; then cover and reduce heat to medium. Cook for 35 minutes.
2. Add the potatoes, bell pepper, and yuca. Cook for another 30 minutes or until the yuca and potatoes are tender.
3. Stir in the giso and cook for another 10 minutes. Stir in the cilantro.

PREPARATION OF GISO

1. Place all of the ingredients in a food processor or blender and process until it makes a smooth paste.
2. Sauté the ingredients in 1 T. of oil for about 10 minutes.

IF YOU GO TO COLOMBIA

Colombians are famed for their hospitality; they are eager to show the diversity of the culture and terrain in their country. Besides the great Amazon River, there is an abundance of other natural wonders to take in. For a good snack, try the corn cakes with cheese.

Chocolate Velvet Soup

Chocolate soup is a luxury rarely found on any menu, but don't let that stop you from trying it at home. This smooth dessert soup might be too rich for large servings, so enjoy smaller servings in little bowls or teacups instead. Whether it is a special occasion or a regular Tuesday, this velvet-textured soup tastes like a celebration.

INGREDIENTS `SERVES 4–6`

4 c.	whole milk
2 or 3 T.	sugar
10½ oz.	bittersweet chocolate, cut into pieces (or 10 ½ squares)
1 T.	butter

TIP Cut chocolate on an angle. It's easier and safer.

VARIATIONS

- Top with fresh sliced bananas or other fresh fruit just before serving.
- Fresh fruit or marshmallows may be threaded onto a stick or served on small plates to be dipped fondue-style into the chocolate soup.
- Serve over cubed pieces of pound cake, or a slice of pound cake on the side.
- Sprinkle with pistachios, sliced almonds, or chopped macadamia nuts.
- Top with a dollop of whipped cream or small scoop of ice cream.

PREPARATION

1. In a heavy, nonstick pan, bring the milk and sugar to a boil over medium heat. Stir constantly to avoid scorching or curdling.
2. Add the chocolate pieces and butter. Use a whisk and stir mixture well until chocolate is completely melted.
3. Remove from heat and cool slightly, if serving warm. The soup should not be served hot because it will be too thin.
4. If serving chilled, let the soup cool to nearly room temperature, then refrigerate for at least 2 hours. The soup will thicken in the refrigerator.

IF YOU GO TO COTE D'IVOIRE

Located on the western coast of Africa, Cote d'Ivoire produces more cocoa than any other country. Also known as the Ivory Coast, the country produces over 40 percent of the world's cocoa beans. French is the official language; but with a very diverse population, more than 60 languages are spoken. Most Ivoirians are able to speak at least two languages fluently. The country has had a long history of storytelling, passing along traditional folktales, myths, and ancestral history from one generation to the next.

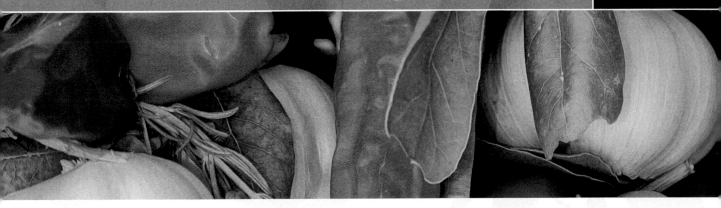

Kohlrabi-Vegetable Soup

Kohlrabi is a mild-tasting tuber that looks like a root vegetable. The bulb is topped with bushy leaves and comes in both light green and purple varieties. This common vegetable in eastern Europe is slowly finding a niche in North America. The flavor has been described as a cross between a radish and a cucumber. The leaves can be utilized in the same way you would prepare kale or collards, but only the bulb is required for this summer vegetable soup. Cut off the top and bottom of the kohlrabi and peel off the outer skin.

INGREDIENTS SERVES 4–6

1 T.	oil
1	medium onion, chopped
2	medium leeks, white and light green parts only, chopped
2 cloves	garlic, minced
3 c.	tomatoes, fresh or canned, including juice; diced
2	large carrots, chopped
2	medium kohlrabies, chopped
2	small zucchini, chopped
1 c.	fresh green beans, cut into 1-inch pieces
5 c.	water
1 c.	frozen peas, thawed
1	handful noodles (or ¾ c. pasta pieces)
1 t.	salt
2 T.	fresh basil, chopped
2 T.	fresh parsley, chopped

PREPARATION

1. In a large pan, heat the oil and sauté the onion, leeks, and garlic for 5 minutes.
2. Stir in the tomatoes, carrots, kohlrabies, zucchini, green beans, and water. Bring to a boil, then cover and reduce heat. Simmer for 25 minutes.
3. Add the peas, noodles, and salt. Cook for another 10 to 15 minutes or until the noodles are tender.
4. Stir in the basil and parsley. Turn off the heat and let the soup rest for 3 minutes.

IF YOU GO TO CROATIA

At social gatherings in Croatia, the women are usually introduced first, followed by the men. Within each group, they are generally introduced by age from the oldest to the youngest. You should not accept second servings unless the host or hostess insists, but you are not obliged to eat more unless you want to. Each village and town has a patron saint. On that particular saint's day, there will likely be a procession and church ceremony. Some villages still have a bonfire as part of the celebration.

Cuban Black Bean Soup

This wonderful soup gets its signature Cuban flavor from the homemade *sofrito,* which you can easily make in your own kitchen. Sometimes referred to as "poor man's soup," most folks find it richly satisfying, especially when served over steamed rice. *This recipe is in honor of Luis and Genoveva Gutierrez.*

INGREDIENTS SERVES 4–6

1 lb.	black beans, soaked at least 12 hours and rinsed
1	bay leaf
1 T.	cumin
1 T.	oregano
3 T.	olive oil
1	onion, diced into chunks
1	red pepper, diced into chunks
1	green pepper, diced into chunks
4 cloves	garlic
1 T.	sugar
2 T.	fresh lemon juice
	salt to taste

GARNISH

½ **c.** cilantro, chopped

PREPARATION

1. In a large stockpot, cover the beans with 2 inches of water. Add the bay leaf, cumin, and oregano.
2. Bring to a boil, then reduce heat and simmer for about 45 minutes or until the beans are tender. Remove the bay leaf.
3. In a separate pan, heat the oil and sauté the onion, red and green peppers, and garlic in the olive oil until soft. Puree in a blender. This is the *sofrito.*
4. Combine the *sofrito,* sugar, and lemon juice with the cooked black beans.
5. Garnish with cilantro, or stir into soup before serving over rice.

IF YOU GO TO CUBA

Cuba is the largest island in the Caribbean, with miles and miles of coastline and beaches. Some say the snorkeling and diving there is the best in the world, with amazing views of fish and underwater coral gardens. Cubans tend to be relaxed and to speak louder than those in some other cultures. They are also known for their love of vibrant colors and music.

White Bean—Tomato Soup

White beans and tomatoes make good partners. Keep these ingredients on hand for a hearty soup that is easy on the budget. With a little planning, you can save time by freezing batches of soaked beans in advance. You could substitute canned beans, but cooking the dried beans from scratch will add more flavor to the soup.

INGREDIENTS SERVES 6–8

2 c.	dried white beans, soaked overnight
10 c.	water
2 T.	olive oil
1	onion, chopped
3	carrots, peeled and sliced
3	stalks celery, sliced
2 c.	tomatoes, fresh or canned, chopped rough
½ c.	tomato paste
2	bay leaves
¼ c.	flat-leaf parsley
1 t.	salt

PREPARATION

1. Soak the beans overnight. Drain the beans, rinse well, and place in a large stockpot.
2. Add the water and olive oil and bring to a boil. Skim off any foam.
3. Add all of the other ingredients, except for the salt. Bring to a boil again.
4. Reduce heat and simmer for 1½ hours or until beans are tender. Add the salt.
5. Serve hot. Pita bread would make a nice accompaniment.

IF YOU GO TO CYPRUS

The people of Cyprus are noted for their friendliness and helpfulness. Cypriots tend to take the attitude that a visit by tourists to their island nation is a compliment. They appreciate hearing what visitors admire and enjoy about their visit to Cyprus. The family is the center of the social structure, stretching to include extended family members. Older people are respected and viewed as wise and experienced. If you are a guest in Cyprus, do not sit down until you are told where to sit. Wait until the hostess has taken the first bite before you begin to eat. You may be offered second and third helpings during dinner, but do not take more than you can eat. It is polite to finish everything on your plate.

Apple-Sauerkraut Stew

The marriage of sweet apples and crisp deli-style sauerkraut creates a wonderfully balanced union. Buy sauerkraut from packages or barrels, not cans, making sure it contains only cabbage and salt. Packaged sauerkraut is often found near the refrigerated pickles or hot dogs in your grocery store.

INGREDIENTS SERVES 6–8

5 c.	vegetable stock
2	stalks celery, chopped
2	large carrots, chopped
2	large apples, peeled, cored, and chopped
2 T.	oil
1	onion, chopped
2 c.	fresh mushrooms
2 c.	sauerkraut, drained
1 T.	caraway seeds, optional
	salt to taste

GARNISH

Sour cream and fresh dill

PREPARATION

1. In a large stockpot, add the vegetable stock, celery, carrots, and apples. Bring to a boil, then reduce to a simmer for 20 minutes or until the vegetables are tender.
2. Heat the oil in a separate pan and sauté the onion, mushrooms, and sauerkraut for 10 minutes.
3. Stir the sauerkraut mixture into the simmering vegetables. Add the caraway seeds if desired. Cook over low heat for 5 to 10 minutes and serve.
4. Garnish before serving if desired.

IF YOU GO TO THE CZECH REPUBLIC

According to the *Guinness Book of World Records,* the Czech Republic has more castles per square mile than any other major country. The largest castle complex in the world is Prague Castle. It was the main residence for a long succession of kings, but since 1918 it has been the main office of the Czech president. When the presidential flag waves above the royal palace, citizens know that their president is in the country. The Český Krumlov Castle, built in the Middle Ages, is the second largest Czech castle, and it is still largely intact. Since the late 1500s, the castle has been protected by bears living in the dry moat. Scores of castles are open to visitors, but beware—many of them still keep bears in the moats.

Apple Pleasure Soup

One of the fundamental aspects of Danish culture is *hygge,* which includes the concept of pleasure coming from comforting, gentle, and soothing things. It is often associated with family and close friends, but it could also refer to candlelight on a rainy night, a picnic in the summer, or perhaps this deep-red soup.

INGREDIENTS `SERVES 4–6`

5	apples, peeled and sliced
1 stick	cinnamon
1	lemon for rind (save the juice)
4 c.	boiling water
6 T.	dry bread crumbs
6 T.	sugar
½ c.	cooking water, reserved from the apples
1½ c.	grape juice, red or purple
4 T.	currant or berry jelly

PREPARATION

1. Put the apples, cinnamon stick, lemon rind, boiling water, and bread crumbs in a large kettle and boil until the apples are tender.
2. Remove the cinnamon stick and lemon rind.
3. Drain the apples and save ½ c. of the cooking water.
4. Press the apples through a sieve.
5. Add the lemon juice, sugar, cooking water, grape juice, and jelly. Stir well, reheat, and serve.

IF YOU GO TO DENMARK

Danes are punctual in both business and social situations, so it is very important to be on time for all appointments. If you are invited to someone's home, check to see if you should remove your shoes. During a meal, your hands should be above the table at all times. An offer to help the hosts in preparation or cleanup would be appreciated. According to the "world map of happiness," created by a social psychologist in England, Danes are consistently happier than people in the rest of the world. If you have a chance, sail Denmark's shoreline for a unique glimpse of the Danish landscape.

Hearty Plantain Soup

When Jason Lee was a student missionary in the Dominican Republic, the cook who prepared the meals where he lodged made many versions of this plantain soup. Now he is a chiropractor in Boise, Idaho, and enjoys serving this specialty to his family.

INGREDIENTS SERVES 4–6

1 T.	oil
2 cloves	garlic, minced
½ t.	salt
½ t.	coriander
½ t.	cumin
8 c.	vegetable stock
2	green plaintains (not ripe)
1	large yuca root
1	large yam or sweet potato

PREPARATION

1. Prepare the vegetables by peeling and dicing them into half-inch pieces.
2. Warm the oil in a large cooking pot. Add the garlic and cook gently until browned.
3. Add the spices and stir until fragrant.
4. Add the stock and remaining vegetables.
5. Cook on medium heat for 15 to 25 minutes, or until vegetables are fork tender.
6. Serve over rice.

IF YOU GO TO THE DOMINICAN REPUBLIC

The communication style in the Dominican Republic tends to be open and direct. It is acceptable to ask personal questions upon meeting someone, but it is best to avoid discussing politics until you know that person better. Humor and laughter are important parts of everyday interaction. Often several generations may live in the same house. Make a point of showing deference to the family elders. If you visit in someone's home, take a gift of flowers or sweets, but avoid the colors black and purple because they are associated with funerals. Gifts in those colors would be considered in bad form.

Peanut-Vegetable Soup

This thick and warming vegetable soup has the added taste and texture of peanuts. Delicious! It has just enough crunch to make this a standout recipe in your repertoire.

INGREDIENTS `SERVES 4–6`

2 T.	oil
1	large onion, minced
2 cloves	garlic
½ t.	red pepper flakes, optional
2	red bell peppers, minced
1½ c.	carrots, chopped
1½ c.	potatoes, peeled and chopped
4	stalks celery, sliced thin
3½ c.	water or vegetable stock
6 T.	peanut butter, crunchy
1 c.	corn kernels
	salt to taste

GARNISH

½ c. peanuts, chopped coarse

PREPARATION

1. Heat the oil in a large pan and sauté the onion and garlic for 4 to 5 minutes. Add the red pepper flakes, if using, and cook for 1 more minute.

2. Add the red bell peppers, carrots, potatoes, and celery. Cook for another 4 minutes, stirring occasionally.
3. Add the water or vegetable stock, peanut butter, and corn, stirring until the peanut butter is thoroughly mixed in. Bring to a boil.
4. Reduce heat, cover, and simmer for about 20 minutes or until vegetables are tender.
5. Sprinkle soup with chopped peanuts before serving.

IF YOU GO TO ECUADOR

Ecuadorians are usually comfortable standing close to one another while talking. If you are included in the conversation, it would be considered impolite to back up or away from the speaker. During conversations, sustained eye contact is expected, even though it may seem a bit unnerving at first. You may not use your finger or hand to point at someone, but you might notice that some Ecuadorians will point by puckering or pursing their lips. If you are presented with a gift, be very demonstrative in your gratitude. Gifts of brand-name chocolate bars from your own country are appreciated. Due to heavy rainfall and high humidity, Ecuador is home to nearly 4,500 species of orchids. In Montecristi, there are hat weavers whose work with straw is so fine, the finished products look like linen.

Pharaoh's Fruit and Filbert Stew

This unusual mix of beans, fruit, and nuts is a tasty break from the usual soup selections offered on restaurant menus. The ingredients have been available for centuries, so it is possible that the pharaohs of Egypt were served something similar. *This recipe is in honor of Hilda Madanat, Heba Antwan, and Nada Malaka.*

INGREDIENTS SERVES 8–10

1 c.	white beans
1 c.	garbanzos
1 c.	barley
1 c.	dried apricots, cut into small pieces
1 c.	currants or raisins
½ c.	figs, cut up (or other dried fruit)
½ c.	sugar, or to taste
11 c.	water
½ t.	salt
½ c.	filberts (also known as hazelnuts), chopped
¾ c.	walnuts, chopped, divided

GARNISH

Walnuts, chopped

PREPARATION

1. Soak the white beans and garbanzos in water overnight. Soak the barley overnight in a separate bowl.
2. Rinse and drain the beans, garbanzos, and barley.
3. Combine all ingredients except the filberts and walnuts. Cook for 50 to 60 minutes or until beans are tender and the fruit is very soft.
4. Stir in the filberts and ½ c. of the walnuts. Remove from heat and cool to room temperature.
5. Refrigerate and serve chilled. Top individual servings with the remaining chopped walnuts.

IF YOU GO TO EGYPT

Once relationships have been established, the general protocol for greeting is to kiss on one cheek and then the other while shaking hands. Men do this with men, and women do this with women. In any greeting between men and women, the woman must extend her hand first. If she does not, a man should bow his head in greeting. If you are invited to an Egyptian's home, take a gift of good quality chocolates or pastries. Do not take flowers because these are usually reserved for weddings or for the ill. When doing business, you can expect a fair amount of haggling, but take care to avoid confrontation. Folks here do not like to say No, so if there is no response, it is usually a negative sign.

EL SALVADOR

Tortilla Soup

Super fast to make, this recipe is perfect for those hectic days when you just want to go home and put your feet up.

INGREDIENTS SERVES 4–6

1 T.	oil
1	large onion, diced
1 clove	garlic, minced
4 c.	vegetable stock
1 c.	water
2	15-oz. cans pinto beans, drained and rinsed
1	15-oz. can red beans, drained and rinsed
1	16-oz. can tomatoes, diced, undrained
1 T.	fresh lime juice
1 bag	tortilla chips, for topping

PREPARATION

1. Heat the oil and fry the onion for 5 minutes or until tender. Stir in the garlic and cook for 2 minutes.
2. Add the vegetable stock, water, pinto beans, red beans, and tomatoes. Heat until the soup simmers.
3. Remove from heat. Stir in the lime juice. Ladle into soup bowls and top with the slightly crushed tortilla chips.

IF YOU GO TO EL SALVADOR

Folks in El Salvador are known for their spirit of goodwill. They are eager to welcome visitors to their country. There are volcanoes and mountains to visit, hot springs and swimming holes to check out, and cornmeal cakes with fresh cheese to try. Visit artists and watch them create paintings and intricate handicrafts. Enjoy lively conversations, and if your timing is right, you can watch turtles hatching at Barra de Santiago.

ENGLAND

Hearty English Cheese Soup

This rich and royal taste experience has to be the ultimate comfort soup. Close your eyes for the first spoonful and savor it for a few seconds. By the time you finish, you'll be flooded with warm memories of whatever made you happy in the past. Take your time and enjoy each spoonful. *Shared by my friend Francis Olsey.*

INGREDIENTS SERVES 4–6

½ c.	margarine
4 c.	milk, low fat
2 T.	cornstarch
24 oz.	sharp cheddar cheese, cubed or grated

GARNISH (optional)

3 hard-boiled eggs, chopped
Vegetarian bacon bits

PREPARATION

1. Melt the margarine in a medium soup pot over low heat.
2. Add in a small amount of the milk, and whisk the cornstarch until smooth. Add the rest of the milk and cook over medium heat, stirring continuously.
3. Cook until bubbly and thickened.
4. Add the cheddar cheese, stirring until the cheese is completely melted. If the mixture is too thick, add small amounts of hot milk until the desired thickness is obtained.
5. Serve with slices of sourdough bread.

IF YOU GO TO ENGLAND

The correct way to eat a scone is to use a knife to cut it in half lengthwise. With the cut sides up, spread them with clotted cream and jam. Eat the scone open-faced, not put together like a sandwich. Visitors can spend days in London, taking in the sights of famous landmarks, royal palaces, and cathedrals. If possible, take a train trip through the countryside. You might see some of the old homes that still have thick, hand-thatched roofs. A walk through a small village will offer an entirely different glimpse of English life.

EQUATORIAL GUINEA

Banana-Mango Soup

It has been said that banana and mango trees grow on practically all the street corners in the cities of Equatorial Guinea. Even if the claim is a slight exaggeration, fruit is prolific and grows easily in this tropical country. If you keep frozen mangoes on hand, this cold soup comes together quickly. Smooth and fruity, it is refreshing on a hot day.

INGREDIENTS SERVES 4–6

2 c.	mango pieces, fresh or frozen
2	medium ripe bananas
2 c.	orange juice
⅓ c.	plain yogurt
⅛ t.	cardamom
1 T.	sugar, optional

PREPARATION

1. Add all of the ingredients to a blender or food processor.
2. Puree until smooth.
3. Taste before serving to see if more sugar is needed.
4. Serve at once, or refrigerate until thoroughly chilled.

IF YOU GO TO EQUATORIAL GUINEA

Located on the west coast of Africa, Equatorial Guinea is the only Spanish-speaking country on the continent; however French is also spoken. Over time, the culture and cuisine have been influenced by Spanish, Portuguese, and Arab immigrants and leaders. People usually identify themselves with a tribal or ethnic connection first, followed by their national identity. Members of the Fang tribe can guide you through a rain forest on foot or by waterway. Rough terrain has spared some forest areas from logging, and the forests continue to remain an important natural habitat to flora and fauna.

Creamy Cabbage Soup

This country-style cabbage soup varies throughout the year, depending on what vegetables are in season. The sweet flavors of fresh garden produce make this simple soup one of the best.

INGREDIENTS SERVES 4–6

1 c.	water
1	small head cabbage, chopped
2	carrots, grated
1	turnip, peeled and grated
2	stalks celery, sliced thin
2 T.	flour
3 c.	nonfat half-and-half (traditional recipe uses 3 c. heavy cream)
2 T.	fresh dill, chopped
	salt to taste

PREPARATION

1. In a large soup kettle, boil the cabbage, carrots, turnip, and celery in the water until almost tender.
2. In a mixing bowl, whisk the flour with the half-and-half.
3. Slowly pour the flour mixture into the boiling soup, stirring constantly. Add the dill.
4. As the soup begins to thicken, lower the heat and simmer until the vegetables are cooked to the desired tenderness.

IF YOU GO TO ESTONIA

In Estonian society, age and experience earn respect. Older people are appreciated for their wisdom. Greetings might seem somewhat formal at first. You should stand when being introduced to someone. Men should initiate greetings with women, and younger people should greet the older person. Always use titles such as Mr., Mrs., or Ms. until you have been invited to use a person's first name. Friendships are very important. Calm conversations, soft voices, and periods of silence are to be expected. Go easy on the compliments. Don't offer one unless it is sincere and genuine; otherwise, the listener will begin to wonder about possible motives.

Mamitu's Potato-Cabbage Stew

Many cooks in Ethiopia take pride in grinding their own spices each day. Others prefer to buy their spices at the local open-air market. No one will be late to dinner when the savory scent of this hearty stew begins to waft from the kitchen. This may be enjoyed on its own or served over couscous. *Mamitu* is an Ethiopian name for "grandmother."

INGREDIENTS SERVES 4–6

4 T.	olive oil
1	large onion, diced
6	carrots, sliced thin
½ t.	salt
½ t.	coriander
½ t.	cumin
¼ t.	turmeric
2 cloves	garlic, minced
½ head	cabbage, shredded
1	15-oz. can diced tomatoes
2 c.	water
2 t.	fresh lemon juice
4	potatoes, peeled and diced

PREPARATION

1. Cook the onion and carrots in olive oil in a large pot over medium heat for 5 minutes.

2. Add the salt, coriander, cumin, turmeric, and garlic. Stir well.

3. Add the cabbage and cook for another 15 to 20 minutes, stirring several times.

4. Stir in the tomatoes, water, lemon juice, and potatoes. Cover and reduce heat to medium low. Cook for 15 to 20 minutes, turning vegetables frequently, or until potatoes are soft.

IF YOU GO TO ETHIOPIA

Ethiopians are hospitable and like to entertain friends in their homes. An invitation to a private home should be considered a great honor. Shake hands with each individual, but not too firmly. The meal begins and ends with ritual hand-washing. Water will be poured over your hands, which are held over a basin. Expect to be urged to take more food. An abundance of food is a sign of generosity and hospitality.

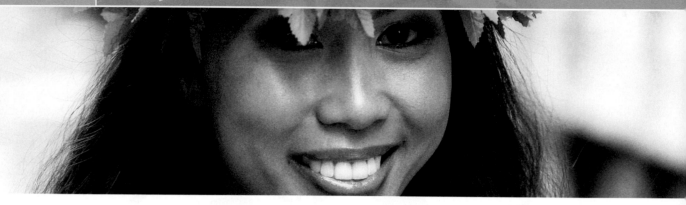

Roasted Carrot and Maple Syrup Soup

Carrots are a dependable staple for most of the globe, including the island country of Fiji. An important crop in Fiji is sugar-cane. This particular recipe calls for maple syrup, an ingredient that is native to North America, but you can use brown sugar if you wish. For convenience, you can make this soup the day before you plan to serve it.

INGREDIENTS SERVES 4–6

5 c.	carrots, peeled and cut into ¾-inch pieces
1 t.	fresh ginger, grated
2 or 3 cloves	garlic, minced
¼ c.	maple syrup (may substitute brown sugar)
2 T.	oil
½ t.	salt
4 c.	vegetable stock
1 c.	water

PREPARATION

1. Preheat the oven to 350°F. Line a roasting pan with nonstick aluminum foil. Combine all ingredients except for the vegetable stock and water, tossing gently to combine.
2. Roast the vegetables for 30 minutes. Stir and turn the vegetables, then continue to roast for another 20 minutes.
3. Place the vegetables in a large pan with the vegetable stock and water. Bring to a boil, then reduce heat and simmer for 20 minutes.
4. Puree the soup in a blender; then return the soup to the pan and reheat.
5. Ladle into bowls or serve in a soup tureen.

IF YOU GO TO FIJI

It has been said that Fijians do not usually swear, especially around foreigners, but they do believe in the power of curses. When greeting one another, a wave with fingers spread wide is customary. Men often greet each other with a prolonged handshake or perhaps a nod of the head. Women often greet each other by kissing the air next to the cheek. To show deep respect to another woman, she may put her nose close to the other woman's nose and cheek and inhale. Folks do not usually point at other people. If they are moving down the road, they may point in the direction they are going to show that they are moving on.

Split Pea Soup

A good split pea soup is hard to beat, but one Finnish tradition makes it even better. Garnish each bowl with a light swirl of mustard just before serving. And if you're not a fan of mustard, just skip that tradition. This soup tastes even better the day after it was made. Split pea soups tend to thicken after they have cooled. Just add a little more water before reheating it.

INGREDIENTS SERVES 4–6

2¼ c.	split peas
8 c.	water
2	medium onions, diced
½ t.	salt
⅛ t.	marjoram
3	stalks celery, chopped
4	medium carrots, chopped
2	medium potatoes, peeled and diced
3 or 4 T.	mustard, American style

PREPARATION

1. Soak the split peas in water overnight. Rinse and drain.
2. Combine the peas, water, onions, salt, and marjoram. Cover and bring to a boil. Simmer for 60 minutes.
3. Add the celery, carrots, and potatoes. Simmer for 30 to 40 minutes, or until vegetables are tender.
4. Before serving, gently add a swirl of mustard on top of each portion.
5. If making soup a day ahead, let the soup cool before refrigerating.

IF YOU GO TO FINLAND

If you love to ski, you'll love the long winter season and the abundance of trails to choose from. If you like saunas, you'll certainly win the respect of Finns. With well over a million saunas, this is a country that takes the bath experience to its highest level. If you are invited to dinner in a Finn's home, you should arrive on time. Accept second helpings if you can, but be sure to eat everything on your plate. When passing the salt, do not hand it directly to someone. Instead, you must place it on the table within that person's reach.

Velvet Green Bean–Parmesan Soup

Whoever thought the plain green bean could be dressed so well? A little attention is all it takes to make this soup special. *This recipe is in honor of Maigan Diop.*

INGREDIENTS   SERVES 4–6

2 T.	olive oil
4 c.	fresh green beans, trimmed (French *haricots vert,* if possible)
1 clove	garlic, crushed
2 c.	vegetable stock
½ c.	Parmesan cheese, grated
¼ c.	milk or half-and-half
	salt to taste

GARNISH

2 T. fresh parsley or dill, chopped

PREPARATION

1. Heat the oil in a medium saucepan. Add the green beans and garlic and cook for 3 to 4 minutes, stirring frequently.
2. Add the stock and your choice of seasonings. Bring to a boil, then lower the heat and simmer uncovered for 15 to 20 minutes until the green beans are tender.
3. Puree the soup in a blender and process until smooth. Return to the pan and reheat slowly.
4. Stir in the Parmesan cheese and milk or half-and-half.
5. Garnish with parsley or dill.

IF YOU GO TO FRANCE

If you are invited to a large dinner party, try to send flowers the morning of the occasion so that they may be displayed that evening. Do not begin to eat until the hostess says, "Bon appétit." Salad is never cut with a knife. Instead, the knife is used to fold the salad onto your fork. (This might take a bit of practice.) The bread is usually placed directly on the table just above your fork. Bread should be broken with your fingers, not cut with a knife. Cheese should be sliced vertically, and the point should never be cut off. Fruit should be peeled and sliced before eating. The French enjoy funny stories and intelligent wit, but they generally do not like to hear or tell jokes. The art museums, architecture, and scenic country drives can keep you occupied for days. Try to visit an open-air market where you can admire the fresh produce and enjoy watching people.

Red Bean and Walnut Soup

The combination of home-cooked beans and chopped walnuts is an unexpected and delicious surprise. Walnuts are a predominant ingredient in vegetarian cooking in the western region of Georgia. This soup offers an uncommonly satisfying taste experience.

INGREDIENTS SERVES 4–6

1½ c.	dried red beans, soaked overnight in water
6 c.	water
2 T.	olive oil
2	medium onions, chopped fine
2 cloves	garlic, minced
½ c.	walnuts, chopped coarse
¼ t.	tarragon
½ t.	coriander
2 T.	fresh lemon juice
1 t.	salt

GARNISH

Fresh cilantro or Italian flat-leaf parsley, chopped

PREPARATION

1. Drain and rinse the soaked beans. Place the beans in a large, heavy pan with the water and bring to a boil. Skim foam if necessary. Reduce heat and cook, loosely covered, until soft, for 60 to 90 minutes.

2. While the beans are cooking, sauté the onions in the oil until golden. Add the garlic and cook for 2 minutes.
3. When the beans are cooked, lightly puree in a blender until coarsely chopped. Do not blend until the texture is smooth. Pour the mixture back into the pan. If it is too thick, add a little water.
4. Stir in the onions and garlic and simmer for a few minutes.
5. Add the walnuts, tarragon, coriander, lemon juice, and salt.
6. Keep the soup warm, at very low heat for about 10 minutes.
7. Ladle into bowls and sprinkle with fresh chopped cilantro or parsley.

IF YOU GO TO GEORGIA

Table manners in Georgia tend to be quite relaxed, although you should try to keep your elbows off the table. Meals are meant to be enjoyed in the company of others. Lively conversation is part of the experience. Even in casual situations, wait to address someone by his or her first name until you have been invited to do so. If you can, find a local market to shop for handmade gifts and souvenirs.

Crock-Pot Potato Soup

Perfect for a Sunday supper, you can throw everything into a Crock-Pot and let it cook while you do other things. *This recipe is in honor of my brother-in-law, Kurt Roeske.*

INGREDIENTS SERVES 4–6

1	medium onion, chopped
2	medium leeks, white part only, sliced
4	medium carrots, chopped
6	medium potatoes, diced
4 c.	vegetable stock
1½ c.	water
1	medium bay leaf
½ t.	salt
¼ t.	nutmeg
½ c.	sour cream, optional

PREPARATION

1. Chop or dice all of the vegetables and place them in the Crock-Pot. Cover with vegetable stock and water.
2. Stir in the bay leaf, salt, and nutmeg.
3. Cover and cook on low heat setting for 8 to 10 hours, or on high heat setting for 4 to 5 hours.
4. Remove the bay leaf. Mash mixture in the Crock-Pot with a potato masher.
5. Stir in the sour cream if desired.

IF YOU GO TO GERMANY

With so many castles, you won't have to travel very far to find one to visit. Tucked away in the mountains, often overlooking pristine lakes or rivers, many are open to the public. Some are still family owned, steeped in tradition, and well worth a visit. Germany has an abundance of hiking trails, but there is a good chance you'll also do plenty of walking in the villages and cities as you take in the sights. If you take a cruise on the Rhine River, look for castles you might not notice from the roadway.

Eggplant-Okra Stew

If you enjoy summer vegetables such as okra and eggplant, be sure to add this stew to your collection of seasonal recipes. Peanuts (also called ground nuts) are a traditional ingredient in the cuisine of many African countries. In this recipe, the peanuts are ground into peanut butter. *This recipe is in honor of Dr. Kwabena Donkor.*

INGREDIENTS SERVES 4–6

1 T.	oil
1-inch piece	ginger, peeled
1	large onion, chopped
¼ c.	tomato paste
6 c.	water
1½ c.	tomatoes, fresh or canned, chopped
⅔ c.	peanut butter
1 t.	salt
1	small chili pepper (or ¼ t. cayenne pepper)
1	medium eggplant, peeled and diced
2 c.	okra, fresh or frozen

PREPARATION

1. In a large, heavy pan, heat the oil and sauté the ginger and onion until the onion is tender.
2. Add the tomato paste and cook over low heat for 5 minutes. Discard the piece of ginger.
3. Add the water and tomatoes and bring to a boil. In a separate bowl, thin the peanut butter with some of the hot water.
4. Reduce heat and add the peanut butter, stirring to blend well. Cook for 5 minutes.
5. Add the salt, chili pepper, eggplant, and okra. Cook until the vegetables are tender. Add more water if needed. The stew should be thick.
6. Serve as is, or ladled over couscous.

IF YOU GO TO GHANA

Ghanaians welcome and respect visitors to their country, especially when international guests show proper decorum. When in the presence of important people or elders, do not sit with your legs crossed. Take care to remove your hat if you are speaking to an elderly person. If you meet a village chief, step forward and bow, but do not shake hands unless he extends his hand. With more than 15 dedicated nature reserves in the country, Ghana provides a natural habitat for more than 800 species of butterflies and more than 700 species of birds. The indigenous art of weaving kente cloth has won worldwide recognition. Detailed patterns have been passed from generation to generation.

Zucchini-Tahini Soup

Keep this recipe handy for zucchini season! When the summer profusion of zucchini or yellow summer squash arrives, you'll be ready for a new way to use this abundant fresh vegetable.

INGREDIENTS SERVES 4–6

2 T.	olive oil
1	large onion, chopped
2 cloves	garlic, minced
4 c.	vegetable stock or onion broth
4	medium potatoes, diced (with or without skin)
2	medium zucchini or yellow summer squash, diced
2 c.	cooked garbanzos, drained and rinsed
½ t.	coriander
2 T.	tahini
	salt to taste

GARNISH

2 t. lemon zest, optional
2 T. parsley, chopped, optional

PREPARATION

1. Heat the oil in a large soup pot over medium heat and sauté the onion until translucent.

2. Add the garlic and stir well.
3. Add the stock and potatoes and bring to a boil. Cook for 10 minutes.
4. Add the zucchini, garbanzos, and coriander. Simmer until vegetables are tender.
5. Stir in the tahini and season to taste.
6. Puree the soup in a blender until smooth. Serve warm or chilled.

IF YOU GO TO GREECE

Greeks are extremely generous hosts and will constantly urge you to eat more, stay longer, or continue with whatever you are doing. The offer is sincere, so if at all possible, do whatever you can to accommodate your host. Mediterranean cuisine offers many wonderful vegetable soups and side dishes to enjoy. More than 1,400 islands make up the Greek isles, but only 169 are inhabited. Visitors like to take boat trips along the coast with short stops at various islands. Be sure to take a good pair of walking shoes for treks in the cities and in the countryside.

GUATEMALA

Fresh Corn Soup

Corn is the basic ingredient in many traditional Guatemalan dishes, especially when it is ground into meal and used to make tamales. But when the sweet corn is fresh from the farm, it is used for special treats like this homemade soup. *This recipe is in memory of Carlos Morales.*

INGREDIENTS `SERVES 4–6`

3	ears of corn
1½ c.	water
2 T.	margarine
1	onion, minced, optional
3 T.	flour
2½ c.	milk
½ c.	liquid from cooking water of corn
	salt to taste

PREPARATION

1. Cut the corn from the cob and cook for 5 to 10 minutes until tender. Drain, reserving ½ c. of the water.
2. Melt the margarine in a large pan. Sauté the onion until it is tender.
3. Add the flour, mixing it immediately.
4. Add the milk slowly, stirring to a smooth consistency.
5. Add the corn liquid from cooking the corn, and seasonings.
6. Bring to a gentle boil, stirring as it thickens.
7. Simmer for 3 to 5 minutes. Serve hot.

IF YOU GO TO GUATEMALA

Most visitors expect to find great photo opportunities at the Mayan archaeological sites. Some of the ancient architecture still exists. The Maya excelled at sculpture, painting, pottery, weaving, and other arts. Today, you can still buy colorful hand-woven fabrics and interesting handicrafts in the local markets. In rural areas, people still wear traditional Mayan dress. The patterns and colors vary from region to region.

Sweet Potato Stew With Dumplings

Sweet potatoes and carrots bring color to this stew, while the curry and nutmeg add exotic flavors. Don't skip the dumplings—they are easy to make and turn this into a special stew.

INGREDIENTS SERVES 4–6

2 T.	margarine
1	small onion, chopped
3 cloves	garlic, minced
1 t.	curry powder
4 c.	vegetable stock
2 c.	water
3	medium carrots, sliced into rounds
4	medium sweet potatoes or yams, peeled and diced
3 T.	flour

DUMPLINGS

1 c.	flour
1½ t.	baking powder
½ t.	salt
½ t.	coriander
2 T.	margarine
7 T.	milk
¼ c.	currants, optional (or other dried fruit, chopped)

PREPARATION

1. Melt the margarine in a large pot over medium heat. Add the onion and cook for 3 minutes. Stir in the garlic and curry powder and cook for 30 seconds.
2. Add the vegetable stock, water, and carrots and bring to a boil. Reduce heat, cover, and simmer for 15 minutes.
3. Add the sweet potatoes or yams and cook for 10 minutes.
4. In a small bowl, place the 3 T. of flour. Take about 1 c. of simmering liquid from the stew and gradually add it to the flour, whisking until it makes a smooth paste. Stir it into the stew to thicken.
5. Place the dumplings on top of the simmering stew, cover, and simmer for 15 minutes.

PREPARATION OF DUMPLINGS

1. In a medium bowl, combine the flour, baking powder, salt, and coriander. Add the margarine and stir lightly with a fork until crumbly.
2. Stir in the milk and currants, if using. Stir with a fork, then use your hands to knead the dough until combined well. Form 1-inch balls.

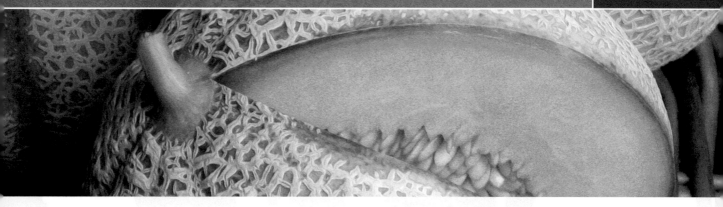

Citrus-Cantaloupe Soup

Legend has it that Christopher Columbus took melon seeds to Haiti in 1493 on his second voyage. No matter who gets the credit, cantaloupe is known to grow well in the Caribbean islands. Here is a refreshing fruit soup to cool you off on a hot day.

INGREDIENTS **SERVES 4–6**

2	medium cantaloupes
½ t.	cinnamon
2 T.	fresh lime juice
2 c.	orange juice

GARNISH

Fresh mint, optional

PREPARATION

1. Slice the cantaloupes in half. Remove the seeds and outer rind. Cut the cantaloupe into cubes.
2. Place the cantaloupe and cinnamon in a blender and puree. Add the lime juice and orange juice, mixing until blended.
3. Chill thoroughly before serving. Garnish with fresh mint if desired.

IF YOU GO TO HAITI

Haitians are known for their outstanding talents as musicians and artists. They have a reputation for performing well and winning international competitions. When negotiating prices for goods and services, savvy shoppers use flair and drama while bargaining for the best deal. Laughter and a good sense of humor play a big role in communication. People tend to use stories and parables before eventually coming to their point. Whistling or pointing at someone is considered rude, but staring at someone is acceptable. Direct eye contact is considered a sign of interest and respect.

HONDURAS

Black Bean—Mango Soup

When mango season arrives, find new ways to use this wonderful fruit. Don't limit them to fruit platters, smoothies, and salsa, but try pairing them with soups like this spicy black bean version.

INGREDIENTS `SERVES 6–8`

1 T.	oil
1	medium onion, diced
2 cloves	garlic, minced
2 c.	water
1	large potato, peeled and diced
2	medium sweet potatoes or yams, peeled and diced
1	medium green bell pepper, chopped
3 c.	tomatoes, fresh or canned with liquid, diced
2	small jalapeño peppers, seeded and chopped
5 c.	black beans, cooked
2	medium mangoes, diced
⅓ c.	fresh cilantro, chopped
½ t.	salt

PREPARATION

1. Heat the oil in a large pan, and sauté the onion for 5 minutes. Add the garlic and cook for another 3 minutes.

2. Add the water and stir in the potato, sweet potatoes, bell pepper, tomatoes, and jalapeños. Bring a boil; then reduce heat to low. Cover and simmer for 10 to 15 minutes or until potatoes are tender but not soft.
3. Stir in the beans and simmer for 5 minutes or until heated through.
4. Stir in the mangoes and cook for 1 minute. Add the cilantro and salt.

IF YOU GO TO HONDURAS

It has been said that the farther you go into the interior of Honduras, the friendlier the welcome. Maybe they don't get as many visitors, or maybe the people are truly happy to see you. Whatever the reason, it is always good to feel at home in new places. Watch for the tapirs that come out to the riverbanks for a drink, and look at the canopy above to spot some of the 400 bird species. You probably won't see a jaguar, but you might spot its tracks if you go into the rain forest with a guide. From May to September, it is possible to spot rare whale sharks along the coast. Be sure to check out some of the ancient cliff carvings.

Chilled Cherry Soup

Hungary may be a small country, but within its borders there is much to enjoy. The landscape ranges from grassy plains to mountains and valleys, dotted by lakes and thermal hot springs. At the end of the day, no matter where you live, a bowl of chilled cherry soup will certainly refresh you.

INGREDIENTS `SERVES 6–8`

3 c.	cherries, pitted, fresh or canned
½ c.	sugar
pinch	salt
	zest of half a small lemon
1 inch	cinnamon stick
5 c.	water
1¼ c.	apple juice
1¼ c.	low-fat sour cream
1	egg yolk
2 T.	flour

PREPARATION

1. Place the cherries, sugar, salt, lemon zest, cinnamon stick, water, and apple juice in a large saucepan. Bring to a boil, then reduce the heat and simmer for 15 minutes.
2. In a bowl, place the sour cream, egg yolk, and flour and mix well.
3. Add a ladleful of the hot soup to the sour cream mixture, mix well, and then add it to the simmering soup while stirring constantly. Simmer for 10 minutes. Do not let it boil.
4. Remove soup from heat. Remove the lemon peel and cinnamon stick, and let the soup cool to room temperature. Once cool, chill well until serving.

IF YOU GO TO HUNGARY

Hungarians put a great deal of emphasis on socializing. Be open and honest in your conversations. Don't be surprised if you are asked personal questions. Feel free to ask about families, leisure activities, and local places of interest. Small talk is also an important prelude to business. Let your Hungarian associates be the ones to steer the conversation to the work topics. Always ask permission before removing your suit jacket at a meeting. If you should receive a gift during your visit, it is expected that you open it immediately.

Split Pea–Rutabaga Stew

The Danes are usually given credit for introducing hardy vegetables such as rutabagas, turnips, cabbages, and potatoes to Icelandic cuisine. These vegetables keep well during cold weather, and they also add good flavor to nourishing soups such as this one. *This recipe is in honor of Daniel and Heidi Weber, who fell in love while serving as student missionaries in Iceland.*

INGREDIENTS   SERVES 6–8

2 c.	yellow split peas
11 c.	water
1	large onion, chopped
1½ t.	dried thyme, rubbed between your fingers
4	medium rutabagas, peeled and cubed
2	large potatoes, peeled and cubed
1 t.	salt

PREPARATION

1. Rinse the split peas well. Bring to a boil in the water. Skim off the foam if necessary.
2. Add the onion and thyme. Reduce heat and simmer, covered, for 45 minutes.
3. Add the rutabagas and potatoes. Simmer for 20 minutes.
4. Add the salt. The soup should be thick. Once it has cooled, additional liquid may be needed before reheating, or it could be served on a plate as a side dish.

IF YOU GO TO ICELAND

The rugged beauty of Iceland includes waterfalls, volcanoes, and winter's natural night show—the aurora borealis. Bundling up in warm blankets and heading outside to watch the colors and patterns of the night sky is a spectacular experience. Icelanders tend to be relaxed and comfortably relate to others on a first-name basis. They can tell you where to find the best thermal hot springs and mineral spas. The Icelandic horse is unique for its sturdy build and heavy coat. Strict laws prevent horses from being imported. Once an Icelandic horse is exported, it is not allowed to return to the country. Excellent souvenirs would be wool blankets, crystal art, and arctic photos. Christmas ornaments are also popular and easy to pack.

Savory Garbanzo Stew

This savory stew is delicious served over rice, but it could also be scooped from your bowl with chapatti or naan, or other types of flat bread. Although it wouldn't be authentic, you could use a steamed flour tortilla if you can't find Indian bread. *This recipe is in honor of Stella Thomas and Shyamala Ram.*

INGREDIENTS   SERVES 4–6

2 T.	oil
1	large onion, chopped
2 cloves	garlic, minced
1 T.	fresh ginger, grated
1 T.	coriander
2 t.	cardamom
3	large tomatoes, diced
2	15-oz. cans garbanzos, undrained

GARNISH

¼ **c.** cilantro, chopped

PREPARATION

1. In a heavy pan, heat the oil and sauté the onion and garlic until light brown.
2. Add the ginger and fry for 2 minutes, stirring constantly.
3. Add the coriander and cardamom, stirring for 2 minutes, or until fragrant.
4. Add the tomatoes and garbanzos with liquid, and cook for 10 minutes or until thick.
5. Garnish with cilantro.
6. Serve over steamed rice.

IF YOU GO TO INDIA

If you visit an Indian home, remove your shoes before entering and wait to be told where to sit. Politely decline the first offer of drinks or snacks. You will be asked again and again if you would like something to eat or drink, but it is part of the protocol to say No to the first invitation. Many foods will be eaten with the fingers, but a tablespoon and fork will be offered if utensils are used. Do not give gifts of leather to Hindus, or gifts of pigskin to Muslims. The sincerity in which a gift is given is very important to the recipient. When you leave a group, you should bid each person farewell individually.

Green Bean–Coconut Soup

No green beans on hand? No problem. Just use carrots, peas, or whatever vegetable you have at hand. Flexibility is important to all good cooks. *In honor of my father, Mel Lyon, who loved living in Indonesia.*

INGREDIENTS SERVES 4–6

2 c.	fresh green beans, cut into ¾-inch pieces
4 c.	water
¼ t.	salt
1⅓ c.	coconut milk
1 T.	oil
1	medium onion, diced fine
2 cloves	garlic, minced
2 T.	peanuts, or other nuts, chopped very fine
1½ t.	coriander
1	medium bay leaf
1 c.	bean sprouts
1 T.	soy sauce
1 T.	fresh lemon or lime juice

PREPARATION

1. Cook the beans in boiling water and salt for 4 minutes.
2. Strain the beans and reserve the cooking water.
3. In a large pan, heat the oil and cook the onion until translucent. Add the garlic and nuts and cook for 2 more minutes, stirring frequently.
4. Add the coriander, the reserved cooking water from the beans, and the coconut milk. Bring to a boil. Add the bay leaf and reduce heat to medium. Cook uncovered for 15 to 20 minutes.
5. Just before serving, add the beans, bean sprouts, soy sauce, and lemon or lime juice.
6. Serve as soon as the soup is hot.

IF YOU GO TO INDONESIA

Indonesians are some of the most charming people you will ever meet. Friendly and hardworking, you will find much to admire about them. While there, you will see towering volcanoes and terraced rice paddies. Folks in rural areas still rely on the strength of water buffalo to assist them with work and transportation. Indonesia is known for its fine batik designs in fabric. Buy several pieces of batik and turn them into pillows or other decorative accents when you get back home. Take in a cultural program if you can, or catch a puppet opera on the street at night.

Pistachio Soup

The largest pistachios are said to come from Iran. Use the best pistachios you can and top with jeweled pomegranate seeds.

INGREDIENTS FOR GARNISH `SERVES 8–10`

1½ T.	oil
½ c.	pistachios, shelled
1½ t.	sugar
1 c.	fresh pomegranate seeds

PREPARATION FOR GARNISH

Heat the oil in a heavy-based pan over medium heat. Add the pistachios and sugar and stir-fry for about 1 minute, stirring constantly. Place the mixture in a small bowl and combine with the pomegranate seeds. Set aside.

INGREDIENTS FOR SOUP

1 c.	pistachios, shelled
6 c.	water, divided
2 T.	olive oil
1 t.	cumin seeds
½ t.	coriander
½ t.	fresh ginger, grated
¼ t.	cayenne pepper
1	medium onion, chopped fine
2	medium leeks, white and light green parts, chopped
2 cloves	garlic, minced
1 c.	rice flour
1 t.	salt
¼ t.	turmeric
1 c.	orange juice

PREPARATION FOR SOUP

1. Grind the pistachios in a blender. Add with 2 c. of the water and blend until smooth. Set aside.
2. Heat the oil over medium heat in a large, heavy pan. Add the cumin and coriander and fry for 30 seconds. Add the ginger, pepper, onion, leeks, and garlic. Cover and cook gently for 5 minutes.
3. Add the rice flour, pistachio puree, remaining water, salt, and turmeric, stirring rapidly with a whisk until it comes to a boil.
4. Reduce heat to low and simmer for 30 minutes, stirring occasionally.
5. Add the orange juice and cook until heated through.
6. Pour into a soup tureen or ladle into individual bowls. Top with pistachio garnish.

IRAQ

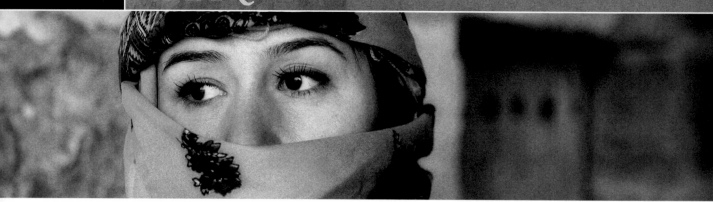

Barley, Lentil, and Fresh Herb Soup

Loaded with fresh herbs, this soup is overflowing with flavor and nutrition. If you don't have the exact amount of fresh dill or other herbs, just use what you have. Tahini is a sesame paste that is found in the international foods aisle of your grocery store or near the imported olives. You could substitute sour cream or plain yogurt for tahini for nearly the same consistency. *This recipe is in honor of Loay Antwan.*

INGREDIENTS SERVES 6–8

2 T.	olive oil
2	medium onions, chopped fine
2 cloves	garlic, minced
½ c.	dried garbanzos
12 c.	water
1 c.	barley
½ c.	dried lentils
2 t.	salt
¼ t.	cayenne pepper
2 c.	tomatoes, fresh or canned
½ t.	turmeric
2 c.	Swiss chard, spines removed, chopped
½ c.	fresh dill, chopped
½ c.	fresh parsley, chopped
½ c.	fresh cilantro, chopped
½ c.	tahini (or sour cream or yogurt)
2 T.	fresh lemon juice

PREPARATION

1. In a large, heavy pan, heat the oil and stir-fry the onions and garlic for 10 minutes or until tender.
2. Add the garbanzos and water and bring to a boil. Reduce heat, cover, and simmer for 40 minutes.
3. Add the barley, lentils, salt, and cayenne pepper and bring back to a boil. Reduce heat and cook for 30 minutes, or until the barley and lentils are tender, stirring occasionally.
4. Add the tomatoes, turmeric, Swiss chard, and fresh herbs. Cover and simmer for 40 minutes. Add the tahini and lemon juice. If the soup is too thick, add warm water a little at a time. Use a potato masher if desired for a coarse consistency.

IF YOU GO TO IRAQ

Hospitality is deeply ingrained in the Arab culture. An invitation to an Iraqi home should be viewed as a great honor and never turned down. Guests are treated to the best food and all of the comforts the host has to offer.

Emerald Isle Oatmeal Soup

Steel-cut oats add a pleasing bit of texture to this fresh-tasting soup. Baby spinach tends to be sweet and tender, so there is no need to remove the stems. Enjoy the rich-green color of this soup while it warms your bones.

INGREDIENTS   SERVES 6–8

4 T.	margarine
3 c.	potatoes, diced
1 c.	carrots, sliced
1	medium onion, sliced
2 c.	fresh white mushrooms, sliced
1 lb.	baby spinach, stems included
4 c.	water or vegetable stock
½ c.	Irish oatmeal (steel-cut oats, not old-fashioned)
	salt to taste

PREPARATION

1. In a large, heavy pan, melt the margarine over low heat. Add the potatoes, carrots, onion, and mushrooms and fry until soft. Stir frequently to avoid browning or sticking to the pan.

2. Add the spinach, water or vegetable stock, and the oatmeal. Stir carefully while spinach wilts down in size. Simmer for 20 minutes. Add seasoning to taste.

IF YOU GO TO IRELAND

The Irish have a solid reputation for working hard, enjoying leisure time, and exchanging local news and gossip. They are also known for going out of their way to welcome visitors to their country. They tend to be calm in a crisis and go about solving problems in a methodical way. The small plate next to your dinner plate is not for bread. Instead, it is used for the peelings removed from boiled potatoes. Take a raincoat and an umbrella—there is a reason Ireland is called the Emerald Isle. Crystal or china made in Ireland would be lovely souvenirs, or you could invest in an article of tweed clothing.

ISRAEL

Matzo Ball Soup

A traditional Jewish recipe handed down through generations, matzo ball soup is still prepared with love, served often, and loved for its comfort. *In honor of Richard and Liliane Elofer.*

INGREDIENTS SERVES 4–6

3	large eggs, beaten lightly
3 T.	olive oil
3 T.	vegetable stock
½ c.	matzo meal
1½ T.	flat-leaf parsley, minced
1½ T.	fresh dill
¾ t.	salt

INGREDIENTS FOR THE BROTH

1	medium onion, chopped
2	stalks celery, chopped
3	medium carrots, sliced thin
1 T.	olive oil
6 c.	vegetable stock
1	medium bay leaf
2 or 3	green onions, including green parts
¼ c.	parsley, chopped
½ t.	salt

PREPARATION

1. To make the matzo balls, stir together the eggs, olive oil, and vegetable stock in a bowl. Add the matzo meal, parsley, dill, and salt, stirring until well combined. Cover and refrigerate for at least 15 minutes and up to 8 hours.
2. Bring a large pot of water to a boil over high heat. Using wet hands, form the matzo dough into 1-inch balls. Carefully drop the balls one at a time into the boiling water. Reduce the heat to low and simmer for 30 minutes until balls are plump and tender.
3. While the matzo balls are simmering, make the soup. Lightly fry the onion, celery, and carrots in olive oil in a large pot for about 5 minutes, or until the vegetables are slightly brown. Add the vegetable stock and bay leaf and bring a boil over high heat. Reduce the heat and simmer for 20 minutes. Stir in the green onions, parsley, and salt; cook for another 10 minutes. Remove the bay leaf.
4. To serve, spoon two or three matzo balls into a bowl and ladle the soup over them.

IF YOU GO TO ISRAEL

With so many biblical landmarks in Israel, you'll see something important wherever you go. Enjoy the teeming markets in Old Jerusalem with Muslim, Christian, and Jewish shops. Choose a special Sabbath platter to use when you get back home.

Bella Bright Minestrone

This minestrone is *bella* because of its bright carrot and tomato colors. But in Italy, minestrone is always *bella* because of its hearty flavor and infinite variations. Endless substitutions with whatever ingredients you have on hand create all kinds of possibilities.

INGREDIENTS SERVES 6–8

2 T.	olive oil
1	onion, chopped
2 cloves	garlic, minced
8 c.	water
1	28-oz. can tomatoes, diced, including juice
3 or 4	potatoes, peeled and diced
2	carrots, sliced
2	stalks celery, sliced
½ c.	barley
1	15-oz. can corn, drained
1	15-oz. can red beans, drained
1	15-oz. can white beans, drained
1 t.	basil
1 t.	oregano
1	bay leaf
	salt to taste

PREPARATION

1. Heat the oil in a large soup pot. Sauté the onion and garlic.
2. Add the water, tomatoes, potatoes, carrots, and celery and cook for 25 minutes.
3. Add the barley and cook for 10 minutes.
4. Add the remaining ingredients and cook for 20 minutes or until the barley is done.
5. Serve hot.

IF YOU GO TO ITALY

In the excitement of being with family and friends, it is customary for Italians to be effusive, expressive, and noisy. People often talk at the same time so they talk loudly in order to be heard. In business and social situations, good topics of conversation include Italian culture, art, food, and family. It is considered impolite to ask someone you have just met about how they make a living; however, this is something that may be revealed in the natural flow of conversation. If you are invited to a meal, bring gift-wrapped chocolates or flowers for the hosts. Children are often named after saints and celebrate their saint's day as if it were another birthday.

JAMAICA

Sweet Mango Soup

With the convenience of frozen mangoes, you can make this spectacular dessert soup during any season of the year. Whether you enjoy it on a hot summer day or a cold winter night, this sweet treat feels like a vacation.

INGREDIENTS SERVES 4–6

4 c.	frozen mangoes, thawed
1 c.	milk
1 c.	plain yogurt
1 c.	coconut milk, unsweetened
3 T.	sugar

GARNISH

2 medium bananas, or substitute other fruit
6 to 8 mint leaves, optional

PREPARATION

1. Puree the mangoes and milk in a food processor or blender.
2. Add the yogurt, coconut milk, and sugar, processing until smooth.
3. Refrigerate for at least 1 hour.
4. Ladle into serving bowls.
5. Garnish with sliced bananas and a mint leaf.

VARIATIONS

You can add ½ t. of fresh grated ginger, or you can omit the sugar and make this a spicy appetizer soup with the addition of a small, finely chopped jalapeño pepper.

IF YOU GO TO JAMAICA

The primary language of Jamaica is English, but it has a distinctive rhythm and charming quality. Conversations also include a sprinkling of Creole, which is a combination of English and African languages. Meals are often served buffet style. Visitors should try as many dishes as possible to demonstrate a gracious spirit. Go easy though, because the spicy heat in some of the items might take you by surprise. It is considered polite to finish everything on your plate. Always use the appropriate greeting for the time of day, such as "good morning," "good afternoon," or "good evening." Try to take at least one boat ride—along the coast, on one of the scenic rivers, or on a subterranean lake to a pirate's cave.

Udon Noodle Soup

Udon is a specific type of Japanese noodle made from wheat flour. It is a thick noodle that is traditionally served with a broth called *dashi* and topped with green onions. Other ingredients, either raw or lightly cooked, can also be used as toppings. The kelp or seaweed adds an authentic flavor to the soup.

INGREDIENTS FOR DASHI SERVES 4–6

6 c.	water
1 piece	dried kelp or seaweed, about 5 inches square

PREPARATION OF DASHI

1. Soak the kelp or seaweed in water for one hour. Bring just to a boil and strain. Discard solids.
2. Set aside until ready to cook udon noodles.

INGREDIENTS FOR UDON

6 c.	dashi stock (as prepared above)
¼ c.	soy sauce
¼ c.	rice vinegar
2 lbs.	fresh udon noodles (found in the produce section of your store)
6	fresh green onions, sliced thin

PREPARATION OF SOUP

1. Bring the dashi, soy sauce, and rice vinegar to a boil in a large stockpot; then add the noodles. Add 1 c. of cold water to the soup.
2. Cook for just a few minutes, or according to the instructions on the package of noodles.
3. Using tongs or a strainer, lift the noodles from the boiling liquid and rinse with cold water. Place the noodles in individual serving bowls.
4. Pour the hot broth over the noodles and top with green onions. Serve at once.

IF YOU GO TO JAPAN

To entice customers, many restaurants in Japan have attractive wax replicas of the dishes on their menu, along with the prices, displayed at the entrance. This is convenient for foreign visitors. All they need to do is point at the dish they would like, and it will be served to them. If you are not led to a table right away, it is safe to assume that you can choose your table. If you choose to sit at a traditional low table, remove your shoes before seating yourself on the *tatami* floor. People typically greet each other by bowing, usually with their arms by their sides. The bow can range from a nod of the head to a 45 degree angle, bending from the waist. If you are seated on a *tatami* floor, you should get on your knees to bow.

Lentil-Vermicelli Soup

There is nothing like the scent of simmering spices, onion, and garlic wafting through the house. Add lentils to the mix, and your family will be asking, "When are we going to eat?" You won't have to call them twice. *This recipe is in honor of Imad Madanat.*

INGREDIENTS `SERVES 6–8`

1½ c.	lentils, rinsed
8 c.	water
1½ t.	salt
½ t.	cumin
1 T.	olive oil
2	medium onions, chopped
3 cloves	garlic, minced
1	small hot pepper, chopped fine
½ c.	cilantro, chopped fine
½ c.	vermicelli (thin spaghetti noodles), broken into small pieces

PREPARATION

1. Place the lentils, water, salt, and cumin in a large stockpot and bring to a boil. Cover and simmer over medium heat for 25 minutes.
2. While the lentils are cooking, heat the oil in a frying pan. Sauté the onions, garlic, and hot pepper over medium heat for 10 minutes, taking care not to let the onions burn or brown.
3. Add the cilantro to the frying pan and stir-fry for 3 minutes.
4. Add the contents of the frying pan and the vermicelli to the lentils and bring to a boil. Cover and simmer over low heat for about 30 minutes, or until the vermicelli and lentils are completely cooked.

IF YOU GO TO JORDAN

From the moment you enter Jordan, to the last moment before you depart, Jordanians will welcome you over and over again. Their generous hospitality and warm spirit inspires you to be a better host or hostess when you return to your home country. The country is filled with biblical landmarks, architectural wonders in Petra, and ancient Roman ruins in Jerash. Along the way, watch for Bedouin families camped here and there. Don't be surprised if you spot a few camels tethered in a parking lot. At the beginning of your trip, be sure to visit a local pastry shop to watch the preparation of sumptuous Arab desserts. Try several of the just-made treats, and vow to stop again for pastries while you are still in Jordan.

Icy Cucumber Soup

This refreshing soup may be served at room temperature or slightly chilled. When it is unbearably hot outside, ice cubes may be added to each individual serving. It has a cooling effect and it tends to make the cucumbers a little crisper. *This recipe is in honor of Chun Moon.*

INGREDIENTS SERVES 4–6

2	large seedless cucumbers (such as English), peeled and sliced paper thin
2 T.	soy sauce
4 t.	rice vinegar or fresh lemon juice
4	green onions, chopped
1 t.	sugar
½ t.	chili powder, optional
1 t.	sesame oil
5 c.	vegetable stock
1 T.	white sesame seeds

PREPARATION

1. Place cucumbers, soy sauce, rice vinegar or lemon juice, green onions, sugar, chili powder, and sesame oil in a large nonaluminum bowl and set aside for 1 hour.
2. Add vegetable stock.
3. Toast sesame seeds in a small pan over medium heat until golden. Set aside to cool. Grind with a mortar and pestle if desired.
4. Serve at room temperature, chilled, or add ice cubes.
5. Top with the sesame seeds.

IF YOU GO TO KOREA

If you are a guest in a Korean home, remove your shoes before you enter the house. It is considered very improper to put your feet on furniture of any kind. Personal space is valued during conversation, but it is difficult to maintain in public areas like the subway or market. Pushing through crowded areas is quite common. It is not usually necessary to apologize for bumping into another person in big crowds when it is unavoidable, especially in urban areas. Koreans will appreciate it if you recognize that their culture, language, and cuisine are unique. Refrain from comparing them to other Asian countries, and enjoy the polite manner in which you will be treated.

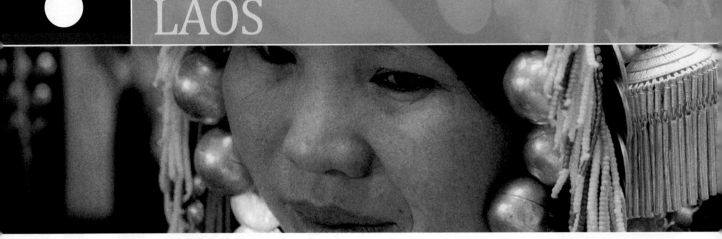

LAOS

Handful Soup

Every country has some version of handful soup. It's one of those dishes where the cook takes a handful of this, a couple of handfuls of that, and eventually it becomes something to eat. Another name for this method might be measureless soup, because there really is no specific recipe. Here are some ingredients that might be used in Laos.

INGREDIENTS `SERVES 4–6`

1 handful per person	noodles
1 pan	water
2 splashes	soy sauce
3 cloves	garlic, sliced
1 block	tofu
3 dashes	oil
Several handfuls	spinach or watercress, chopped rough
Couple of handfuls	bean sprouts
1 or 2 handfuls	cilantro, chopped
1 bundle	green onions, chopped

PREPARATION

1. Cook the noodles in the water and soy sauce until the noodles are tender.
2. While the noodles are cooking, slice the garlic and dice the tofu. Fry together until the tofu turns golden.
3. In individual bowls, distribute the spinach or watercress, bean sprouts, and cilantro.
4. Distribute the cooked noodles and cooking water in the bowls, followed by the tofu and garlic.
5. Top each bowl with the onions.
6. Add extra soy sauce if needed.

IF YOU GO TO LAOS

Someone once described Laotians in poetic terms as people who are so in tune with their surroundings, they are able to hear the rice grow. They are known to be patient and calm. In this Buddhist country, there is no shortage of temples to visit. If you see a pile of shoes at the entrance of a temple, business, or shop, take care to remove your own before entering. On buses, seats are often given up for monks. A woman should never touch a monk. If she has an offering or a gift, she should place it within a monk's reach so he can pick it up himself. A person's head is considered sacred, so refrain from touching anyone, including children, on the head.

Tomato-Basil Soup

Tomatoes just picked from the garden always taste best, but you can still serve a good tomato-basil soup by substituting a canned variety. Here is a quick-and-easy recipe to enjoy when you are short on time or when unexpected visitors stop by.

INGREDIENTS SERVES 4–6

1 T.	olive oil
1	small onion, chopped
1 clove	garlic, minced
1	28-oz. can diced tomatoes, including juice
1½ to 2 c.	water
1	6-oz. can tomato paste
2 T.	fresh basil, cut into thin strips, or ½ t. dried basil
	salt to taste

PREPARATION

1. Heat the oil in a large saucepan. Sauté the onion and garlic until onion is tender.

2. Add the tomatoes, water, and tomato paste. Stir until smooth, and then add the basil. Bring to a boil, and immediately reduce heat to low. Simmer for 15 minutes.

3. Adjust seasonings or add water to desired taste and consistency.

IF YOU GO TO LATVIA

One of the distinguishing features of Latvian culture is the folk song, which is also considered to be a national treasure. After sharing a meal, it is common to gather for singing. It would be very unusual to meet someone in Latvia who has never been a member of a choir. If you fall in love while you are in Latvia, do not declare yourself by sending a dozen red roses. Red roses are associated with funerals. While dining, napkins should be kept on the table, not placed in your lap.

LEBANON

Lentil, Bean, and Bulgur Stew

This hearty bean stew is so delicious, it is well worth the effort to use dried beans and cook them from scratch. Cooks from Lebanon would likely use more lemon juice than this recipe specifies, but you can add more according to your own taste. *This recipe is in honor of Asmahan Antar and Berge Kiraz.*

INGREDIENTS SERVES 6–8

½ c.	dried white kidney beans (cannellini)
½ c.	dried red kidney beans
½ c.	dried garbanzo beans
¼ c.	dried baby lima beans
¼ c.	lentils
7 c.	water
2 T.	olive oil, divided
1	medium bay leaf
1	medium onion, diced
2 cloves	garlic, minced
¼ c.	bulgur
½ c.	rice
1 t.	cumin
1 t.	salt
1 T.	fresh lemon juice

PREPARATION

1. Soak all the beans and lentils in plenty of cold water overnight, or for at least 8 hours.
2. Drain and rinse well.
3. Place the beans, lentils, water, and 1 T. olive oil in a large pan and bring to a boil. Skim off foam if necessary and discard. Cook over medium-high heat for 5 minutes; then reduce the heat to medium low. Add the bay leaf and cook for 45 minutes or longer until the beans are nearly tender.
4. In a separate pan, heat the 1 T. olive oil and sauté the onion and garlic and set aside.
5. Add the onion, garlic, bulgur, rice, cumin, and salt. Cook for 20 minutes. Stir frequently so that the grains don't stick to the bottom of the pan. Add more water if needed.
6. When the beans, bulgur, and rice are tender, add the lemon juice and cook for 3 minutes.

IF YOU GO TO LEBANON

You will find people in Lebanon to be outgoing, courteous, and welcoming. Greetings are important preludes to any interaction and usually include inquiries about family. Meals are rarely eaten alone.

Black-Eyed Pea Soup

Black-eyed peas are a favorite staple in all of the regions of western Africa. Ingredients vary according to the vegetables available. This will make a nice stew to serve over polenta or grits.

INGREDIENTS   SERVES 6–8

1 c.	dried black-eyed peas, soaked in water overnight
2 T.	oil
2 cloves	garlic, peeled
2	onions, chopped
1 c.	celery, diced
6 c.	water
1 pinch	cayenne pepper
1 pinch	thyme
¾ t.	allspice
1 c.	corn, fresh or frozen (optional)
1 c.	okra, fresh or frozen (optional)
2 c.	fresh spinach, chopped
3 c.	diced tomatoes, fresh or canned
¾ t.	salt

GARNISH

1 T. fresh cilantro, chopped

PREPARATION

1. Soak the black-eyed peas in water overnight. Drain and rinse well. Set aside.
2. Heat the oil and sauté the garlic, onions, and celery for 5 minutes.
3. Add the water and black-eyed peas. Bring to a boil, reduce heat, and simmer for 30 minutes.
4. Add the spices, corn, and okra (if you are using them), spinach, tomatoes, and salt.
5. Simmer for another 30 minutes or until the black-eyed peas are tender.
6. Top each bowl with chopped cilantro.

IF YOU GO TO LIBERIA

It is important to say Hello to people you pass in the street. As a foreigner, you may be expected to shake hands with perfect strangers. Greetings often consist of a handshake and a finger snap. As you grasp the other person's hand, let your hand slide until just your fingertips are touching. Then snap your middle fingers simultaneously with the other person. With a little practice, a resounding snap can be produced.

Cauliflower-Onion Soup

For the best flavor, choose a very fresh cauliflower. Cauliflowers that have been stored for a longer period of time have a stronger taste. This soup can be served thick and chunky, but when it is pureed, the flavors are subtle and smooth.

INGREDIENTS   SERVES 6–8

2 T.	oil
2 c.	onions, chopped
2 c.	potatoes, peeled and diced
1½ t.	cumin
1½ t.	dry fennel
4 c.	hot water
1 cube	bouillon
5 c.	cauliflower florets (about one medium-sized cauliflower)
2 T.	fresh lemon juice
¾ t.	salt

GARNISH

1 medium tomato, chopped
2 green onions, white and light green parts, sliced thin

PREPARATION

1. In a large stockpot, heat the oil and sauté the onions for 5 to 10 minutes, or until onions are tender.
2. Add the potatoes, cumin, and fennel. Stir and cook for 1 minute.
3. Add the hot water and bring to a boil.
4. Add the bouillon cube and cauliflower. Lower heat, cover, and simmer for 10 minutes or until vegetables are tender.
5. In a blender, puree the mixture in small batches until smooth.
6. Add the lemon juice and salt, and slowly reheat.
7. Serve hot.
8. Garnish with chopped tomatoes and green onions.

IF YOU GO TO LIBYA

Traditionally, men and women eat in separate rooms. If there is only one room, one group will take their meal first, followed by the second group. In large urban areas, it is becoming more common for men and women to eat in the same room. In some areas, a bowl of perfumed water will be brought around the table before the meal. Dip three fingers of your right hand in the water as a form of ritual cleansing. Eat only with the right hand. The Libyan Desert, which is part of the Sahara, contains some mountains and several oases. Visit the ornate Gurgi Mosque in Tripoli to see Islamic architecture with Italianate influences.

LIECHTENSTEIN

Almond-Buttermilk Soup

Throughout the generations, folks have relied on their own milk cow to sustain them. Today dairies are the main providers of dairy products, including buttermilk. This updated version of buttermilk soup is quite special. It is best when served very cold.

INGREDIENTS   SERVES 4–6

1 c.	blanched almonds, slivered
1½ c.	dried bread crumbs
2 cloves	garlic, chopped
1 t.	orange zest
1 T.	lemon juice
4 c.	buttermilk, divided
½ c.	orange juice
1 t.	salt

GARNISH

1 T. parsley, chopped

PREPARATION

1. Place the almonds, bread crumbs, garlic, orange zest, lemon juice, and 1 c. of the buttermilk in a blender. Process until smooth, adding more of the buttermilk if the mixture becomes too thick to blend.
2. Pour into a large bowl and add the remaining buttermilk, orange juice, and salt.
3. Stir and refrigerate until cold.
4. Ladle into bowls and garnish with chopped parsley.

IF YOU GO TO LIECHTENSTEIN

Liechtenstein, the small principality sandwiched between Switzerland and Austria, is a double landlocked country. Landlocked countries have no coastline, but, in this case, the countries surrounding Liechtenstein are also landlocked. Many tourists cross the border to visit the post office. The postage stamps are famous for their artistic designs and bright colors. The Postage Stamp Museum in Vaduz is filled with foreign visitors every day.

Chilled Beet Soup

Fresh beets are sweeter and brighter than canned beets and worth the extra time and effort to prepare. You can cook the beets the day before you plan to assemble the soup, if you wish. This soup is traditionally served with a side of fried potatoes with onion and fresh dill. Sometimes the fried potatoes are served as a garnish on top of the soup. Either way, the combination is fabulous.

INGREDIENTS SERVES 4–6

8 to 10	medium beets
10 to 12 c.	water
2	medium seedless cucumbers, peeled and chopped
¼ c.	fresh dill, chopped
2 T.	apple juice
2 T.	fresh lemon juice
½ t.	salt
2 c.	light sour cream

PREPARATION

1. Clean the beets well and place them in a large pan. Add 10 cups of water, or more if needed, to cover the beets. Bring the water to a boil, then simmer uncovered for 20 minutes or until just tender.

2. Lift the beets from the pan and put them in a colander to cool. Strain the cooking water into a large bowl or container, saving at least 10 c. for the soup. Set the beets aside until cool.

3. Peel and shred the beets. Combine the beets, cucumbers, dill, apple juice, lemon juice, salt, and sour cream with the reserved cooking water. Chill for several hours.

4. Serve with fried potatoes, onion, and dill if desired.

IF YOU GO TO LITHUANIA

Some of the most loyal basketball fans can be found in Lithuania. The games are followed closely and discussed at great length. Depending on the weather, you might want to take a hot-air balloon ride over the orthodox churches and spires of the capital city of Vilnius. Ice fishing is a winter pastime, but, with a little luck and skill, it can put dinner on the table for some fishermen and their families.

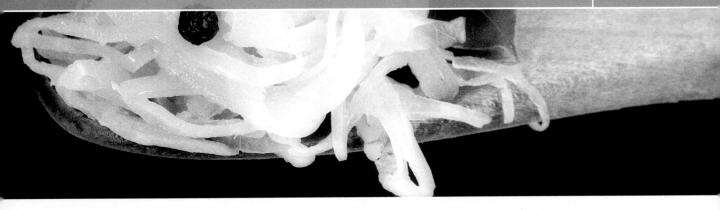

Creamy Green Bean–Potato Soup

Potatoes add substance and flavor, while the green beans provide color and flavor of their own. Many variations of this delicious soup are possible. Enjoy it as it is, or toss in a few mushrooms or a diced summer squash.

INGREDIENTS SERVES 6–8

3 T.	margarine
1	small onion, chopped
4 c.	water
6	medium potatoes, peeled and diced
3 c.	green beans (fresh or frozen), chopped
2 c.	light cream
¾ t.	salt
	paprika

PREPARATION

1. In a small skillet, heat the margarine and sauté the onion in margarine until tender. Set aside.
2. In a large, heavy pan, bring the water to a boil. Add the potatoes and cook until starting to soften.
3. Add the green beans; simmer until potatoes and green beans are tender.
4. Drain about half of the water. Add the light cream and onion. Adjust seasonings to taste.
5. Simmer until heated through, but don't let it boil.
6. Ladle into individual bowls and sprinkle with paprika.

IF YOU GO TO LUXEMBOURG

Folks in Luxembourg tend to be somewhat reserved and formal with outsiders, relaxing only with family and close friends. Even then, private matters are usually kept with the family. Table manners are traditionally Continental. Food is eaten with a knife and fork, including sandwiches. It is polite to finish everything on your plate. Outdoor enthusiasts love Luxembourg for its well-marked hiking and biking trails. The Wenzel Circular Walk, also described as "1,000 Years in 100 Minutes," is a historical tour of Luxembourg City. Visit the Bock Casemates, a UNESCO World Heritage Site, and walk through its tunnels and fortifications.

MADAGASCAR

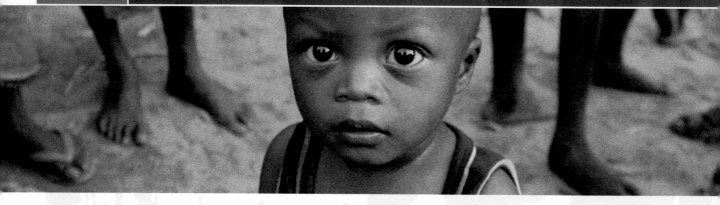

Vanilla Bean–Pumpkin Soup

Madagascar leads the world in vanilla production, where it is highly prized for its quality and taste. Vanilla extract can be substituted for the vanilla bean pods in this recipe, but take care to add just a little at a time so that it doesn't leave a bitter taste. The vanilla flavor should be subtle—present but not overpowering.

INGREDIENTS SERVES 4–6

4 c.	water
1	15-oz. can pumpkin puree (not the pre-spiced puree intended for pie)
¼ t.	salt
1 c.	milk
2	vanilla bean pods, split lengthwise
1 c.	light cream

PREPARATION

1. In a large pan, mix the water, pumpkin, and salt and bring to a slow simmer.
2. In a separate small pan, bring the milk just to a boil. Remove from the burner and set aside.
3. Add the split vanilla bean pods to the milk and let them infuse for 20 minutes.
4. Remove the pods from the milk. Scrape the inside of the pods with a teaspoon or knife, transferring the tiny beans back to the milk. Whisk until the tiny beads of vanilla beans are evenly distributed throughout the milk.
5. Add the cream to the milk and stir.
6. Combine the milk-and-cream mixture with the pumpkin mixture.
7. The soup will be somewhat thin, so you might prefer to serve the soup in small teacups. It will be easier to sip the soup than to use a soupspoon and bowl.

IF YOU GO TO MADAGASCAR

A trip to visit Madagascar, the fourth largest island in the world, would not be complete without visiting at least one wildlife park. Where else could you be entertained by so many species of lemurs swinging through the trees? Listen for a concert of jungle calls as they vocalize with each other. The rain forests are lush with ferns, orchids, and moss-covered branches. Madagascar is sometimes described as an island forgotten in time; visitors will appreciate the mountains, desert plains, and famous coral reefs. Avoid wearing military-style clothing as it could lead to misunderstandings and arrest. People tend to stand close together when conversing. If you back up while someone is talking to you, it will be assumed that you don't like them. Look for good quality vanilla, cinnamon, and cloves to take back home.

Creamed Cabbage Soup

This simple soup is so delicious. It only has two main ingredients, so you might not have to stop at the store on your way home. Warm and comforting, it can only be improved with a side of corn bread. *This recipe is in honor of Gordon and Cheryl Doss.*

INGREDIENTS SERVES 4–6

1	small head cabbage
4 c.	water (enough to cover the cabbage)
3 to 4 c.	milk (if you like a richer taste, exchange 1 c. of cream for 1 c. of the milk)
¼ t.	salt

PREPARATION

1. Chop the cabbage finely. Discard the core or any tough portions of the leaves.
2. Add water to cover and simmer until tender.
3. Drain off all but about 1½ c. of the water.
4. Add the milk and salt. Stir frequently until the soup is hot, but do not bring it to a boil.
5. Serve with corn bread if desired.

IF YOU GO TO MALAWI

One of the main staples of the Malawian diet is boiled cornmeal, generally eaten twice a day. It is usually served for lunch and dinner, either as a simple meal by itself or along with stew. Cornmeal is generally preferred over rice and potatoes. The diverse landscape of Malawi is home to at least nine national parks and wildlife reserves. The most common animal in this country is said to be the hippo, which has become the unofficial symbol of Malawi wildlife. They are especially plentiful in the Shire River at the Liwonde National Park. Casual observers will enjoy spotting a variety of birds, but serious birders can record more than 200 species in just a couple of days.

MALAYSIA

Baby Bok Choy—Cashew Soup

Baby bok choy is sweeter than adult varieties. Many Asian soups are made by preparing a broth separately from the main ingredients. The broth is ladled over stir-fried vegetables or noodles, but it doesn't completely cover the vegetables. Sometimes cooks make extra broth to be used the next day over entirely different ingredients. *This recipe is in honor of Millie Voon.*

INGREDIENTS FOR THE BROTH SERVES 4–6

4 c.	water
2 T.	soy sauce
½ t.	fresh ginger, grated
½ t.	sesame oil

INGREDIENTS FOR THE BASE

2 T.	oil
2	medium leeks, white part only, sliced lengthwise, then into half-moon shapes
3 cloves	garlic, minced
¾ c.	cashews (may substitute peanuts)
2	bunches baby bok choy, rinsed well, cut in half lengthwise
1 t.	sesame seeds

PREPARATION

1. Use a medium pan to make the broth. Heat the water, soy sauce, ginger, and sesame oil just until it reaches a boil.
2. In a large frying pan or wok, heat the oil and sauté the leeks and garlic over medium-high heat for 2 minutes.
3. Add the cashews and cook for 1 minute.
4. Add the bok choy. Cover and cook for 4 minutes, stirring once. (The bok choy will wilt down, similar to spinach.)
5. Remove the cover, stir again, and cook for 2 minutes or until the bok choy is just cooked.
6. Using tongs, place the bok choy mix into individual bowls. Ladle hot broth over the vegetables and serve. Do not cover the vegetables completely with the broth. Sprinkle with seasame seeds.

IF YOU GO TO MALAYSIA

Malaysia has become a cultural melting pot with many distinct traditions according to people's religion and country of origin. Gifts of sweets, along with a souvenir from your home country, are greatly appreciated.

MEXICO

Pozole

Perfect as a full meal, pozole (pronounced *poh-SOH-leh*) is thick and hearty. Hominy is the most traditional ingredient in the base, but the fresh vegetables that top the cooked soup can vary considerably. This is usually a Christmas favorite in Mexico. *This recipe was inspired by Magarita Neyra.*

INGREDIENTS SERVES 6–8

1 T.	oil
1	medium onion, chopped fine
1½ c.	chicken-style meat substitute, drained and rinsed, sliced thin
4 c.	vegetable stock
1 c.	water
1	15-oz. can hominy, drained and rinsed
1 c.	green enchilada sauce

TOPPINGS

- Shredded lettuce
- Avocados
- Radishes
- Onions
- Cilantro
- Jalapeño peppers
- Lime wedges

PREPARATION

1. In a large, heavy pan, heat the oil and sauté the onion for 3 minutes.
2. Add the chicken-style meat substitute, frying until nicely browned.
3. Add the vegetable stock and water and bring to a boil. Reduce heat to medium.
4. Add the hominy and green enchilada sauce. Simmer for 5 minutes.
5. Ladle into individual bowls. Allow guests to add their own toppings to the soup.
6. Serve with warm tortillas on the side.

IF YOU GO TO MEXICO

Mariachi bands are internationally loved for their joyful music. Mexicans tend to be fun-loving, hard working, and devoted to family. If you receive an invitation to a Mexican home, plan to arrive about 30 minutes later than the specified time; otherwise you could be perceived as being overeager. If you receive a gift, you should open it immediately and react enthusiastically. A gift from the region of your home country is appreciated.

Red Soup

Endless variations of this traditional Moldovan soup are possible. As long as beets and tomatoes are included, it will be a red soup. This version is hearty, filling, and tastes even better the day after it has been prepared. Enjoy it with a thick piece of bread.

INGREDIENTS `SERVES 8–10`

2 T.	oil
2	medium carrots, diced
1	medium onion, chopped
2 cloves	garlic, chopped
8 c.	water
2 c.	cooked beets, diced (canned beets may be used)
4 c.	white cabbage, shredded
2	medium potatoes, peeled and diced
3 c.	tomatoes, fresh or canned, chopped
1 t.	salt
2 T.	fresh basil, shredded

PREPARATION

1. Heat the oil and sauté the carrots, onion, and garlic until the carrots are tender.

2. Add the water and beets and bring to a boil. Stir in the cabbage, potatoes, tomatoes, and salt. Reduce the heat and simmer for 30 minutes or until the potatoes are tender.

3. Just before serving, add the basil.

IF YOU GO TO MOLDOVA

If you are a dinner guest in a Moldovan home, do not choose your own seat at the table. The hosts may have a particular seating plan in mind, so wait to be told where to sit. Do not place your napkin on your lap, but keep it visible on the table at all times. Newlyweds tend to live with the groom's parents until they are able to find a place of their own. In villages, there is a general rule that the youngest son and his family will live with his parents. Upon their death, he will inherit the contents of the house. Graveyards are visited often to pay respect to deceased loved ones. Wine is customarily poured on the graves.

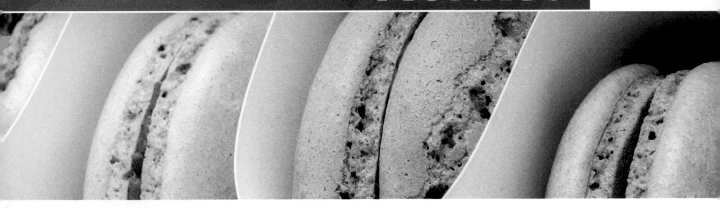

Corduroy Carrot Soup

This golden soup could be proudly served to either royalty or peasants. For the best flavor, be sure to use fresh, not frozen, carrots.

INGREDIENTS SERVES 4–6

2 T.	oil
1	large onion, chopped fine
4 c.	carrots, peeled and sliced thin
5 c.	vegetable stock
1 to 2 T.	tomato paste
¼ c.	white rice, uncooked
¾ t.	salt
⅔ c.	milk or cream

GARNISH

Croutons and grated Gruyère cheese

PREPARATION

1. In a large stockpot, heat the oil and sauté the onion over medium heat. Stir occasionally until onion is tender but not browned.
2. Add the carrots, vegetable stock, tomato paste, and rice. Simmer uncovered for 30 minutes until the carrots are tender and the rice is cooked.
3. In small batches, puree the soup in a blender. If desired, allow small bits of carrots to remain in the soup for color.
4. Return the soup to the stockpot. Add the salt and stir in the milk or cream. Bring the soup back to a low simmer.
5. Remove from heat and serve into a tureen or individual soup bowls.
6. Garnish if desired.

IF YOU GO TO MONACO

Monaco occupies a little less than one square mile, which makes every square inch of real estate extremely valuable. With its high-rise buildings towering above the port, it might seem more like Manhattan than Mediterranean. Three sides of this tiny country are bordered by France while the fourth borders the Mediterranean Sea. The city of Monte Carlo overlooks a sparkling harbor filled with the yachts of millionaires. French and English are both spoken here, but it is considered ill-mannered for the speaker to switch from one language to another in the same conversation.

Broccoli-Tofu Soup

Simple and nutritious, this soup can be stretched by adding more water, or made chunkier by reducing the water. Prepare all of the vegetables before you begin to ensure that the colors will be fresh and bright and the broccoli and zucchini will not be overcooked.

INGREDIENTS SERVES 4–6

1 lb.	tofu, diced
1 t.	sesame oil
3 t.	vegetable oil
2 T.	hoisin sauce
2 T.	soy sauce
1 t.	fresh ginger, grated
1½ c.	broccoli florets
2 c.	Chinese cabbage, shredded
2	small zucchini, halved lengthwise, sliced
5 c.	water
2 T.	cilantro leaves, chopped fine

PREPARATION

1. Place the tofu in a large pan. Mix the sesame oil, vegetable oil, hoisin sauce, soy sauce, and fresh ginger. Pour over the tofu and stir carefully to combine. Let marinate while preparing the vegetables.
2. Cut the broccoli into florets and set aside.
3. Shred the cabbage and set aside.
4. Slice the zucchini and set aside.
5. Pour water over the tofu and bring to a boil. Add the broccoli and cook for 2 minutes.
6. Add the zucchini and cook for 2 minutes.
7. Add the cabbage and cook for 2 minutes.
8. Add the cilantro and serve immediately.

IF YOU GO TO MONGOLIA

Gift giving is not considered necessary in Mongolia, but it does help to generate good feelings. In most cases, gifts are tokens that represent the visitor's home country or something that might be considered interesting. Appropriate gifts could be baseball caps with sports logos or other items emblazoned with something of regional importance. Gifts are usually opened in front of other people to show that goodwill has been established. Visitors should be neat and clean, not appearing to be unshaven or wearing rumpled clothing. A relaxed approach to punctuality is common because it is understood that you will visit with people along the way to an appointment. Taking joy in the moment is considered the norm because tomorrow is always an opportunity to finish what couldn't be done today.

Roasted Eggplant and Tomato Soup

Roasting vegetables brings out sweet and smoky flavors that can't be achieved by any other method. If you prepare the vegetables ahead of time, you can put this soup together in just a few minutes before serving time.

INGREDIENTS — SERVES 8–10

3	medium eggplants, halved lengthwise
6	medium tomatoes, halved and cored
¼ c.	extra virgin olive oil, divided
1 entire bulb	garlic
1	medium onion, chopped fine
½ c.	tomato paste
6 c.	vegetable stock
¾ t.	oregano
½ t.	salt

GARNISH

½ **c.** olives, sliced or chopped

PREPARATION

1. Preheat the oven to 425°F. Brush the eggplants and tomatoes with olive oil. In a rimmed baking pan, arrange eggplant halves, cut sides down. Arrange the tomato halves cut side up. Use a second pan if necessary.
2. Cut off the top ¼ inch of the garlic bulb. Brush the top with olive oil. Wrap in foil and add to the pan of vegetables.
3. Roast vegetables for 45 minutes or until tender and browning in spots. Let stand for 20 minutes or until cool enough to handle. Peel the vegetables and discard the skins. (You can store the vegetables in an airtight container in the refrigerator for up to 3 days.)
4. In a large, heavy pan, heat the remaining olive oil and sauté the onion for 10 to 12 minutes or until tender.
5. Stir in the tomato paste and cook for 2 minutes.
6. Add the eggplant and tomatoes. Squeeze the roasted garlic pulp onto the vegetables and stir to combine.
7. Stir in the vegetable stock, oregano, and salt.
8. Puree in a blender. Return to pan and reheat.
9. Serve in individual bowls, topped with olives.

IF YOU GO TO MONTENEGRO

Situated on the deep blue waters of the Adriatic Sea, Montenegro attracts visitors from all over the world. The Ostrog Monastery, carved into the mountain cliffs, is one of the most visited shrines of the Christian world. This small republic has rivers, coastlines, canyons, and forests. It maintains a fine reputation for its artistic and cultural heritage.

MOROCCO

Carrot Soup With Cilantro Drizzle

This delicious combination of carrots and spices may tempt you to refill your bowl for a second serving. If you are short on time, prepare this soup the day before you intend to serve it. It can be served just as it is, but the Cilantro Drizzle transforms it into something spectacular.

INGREDIENTS **SERVES 4–6**

1 T.	olive oil
1	small onion, chopped
1	medium leek, white part only, sliced in thin rounds
1 clove	garlic, minced
2 t.	fresh ginger, grated
7	large carrots, sliced thin
¼ t.	turmeric
½ t.	cumin
½ t.	paprika
4 c.	water or vegetable stock
	salt to taste

Cilantro Drizzle Puree these ingredients in a blender until smooth. Set aside.

1 c.	fresh cilantro leaves
1 clove	garlic, minced
¼ t.	cumin
¼ t.	paprika

3 T.	olive oil
3 T.	lemon juice

PREPARATION

1. Heat the oil in a large saucepan and sauté the onion for 4 minutes. Add the leek, garlic, ginger, and 2 T. of water or vegetable broth. Cook 4 minutes until the onion and leek are tender.
2. Stir in the carrots, turmeric, cumin, paprika, and water or stock. Bring to a boil, then reduce heat and simmer for 35 minutes or until carrots are very soft. Remove from burner and let cool for 10 minutes.
3. Puree the soup in a blender until smooth. Return to saucepan and slowly reheat.
4. Ladle the soup into bowls. Lightly swirl a spoonful of Cilantro Drizzle over each serving.

IF YOU GO TO MOROCCO

If you are invited to a Moroccan home, take along a gift of pastries, dates, or nuts for the hosts. When there is a large group of people at a social function, first greet those on your right, followed by those on your left.

Burmese Stacked Soup

In traditional Burmese homes, families eat their meals at a low table while sitting on a bamboo mat. A typical meal would include steaming hot rice as a staple. Out of respect, the eldest diners are always served first. Even when the elders are absent, the first morsels of rice are scooped up and set aside as an act of respect to one's parents. *This recipe is in honor of Andrew and Lisa Myaing.*

INGREDIENTS SERVES 4–6

2 c.	red lentils
6 c.	water
¼ c.	cilantro, chopped
	salt to taste

PREPARATION

1. Bring lentils and water to a boil in a large pan. Reduce heat to medium and cook until the lentils lose their shape and make a thick porridge.
2. Stir in the chopped cilantro and season with salt.
3. While the lentils are cooking, prepare the garnishes.

GARNISHES

2 green chili peppers, cut into rings and soaked in water and lemon juice for one hour
2 c. chopped sweet onions, sautéed slowly until dark and caramelized
2 potatoes, peeled and grated, fried until crisp and golden, drained on paper towels
2 c. bread cubes, fried or toasted
1 c. cilantro, chopped

After the soup has been ladled into individual bowls, the diners can stack their soup with garnishes according to their tastes.

IF YOU GO TO MYANMAR

Myanmar, also known as Burma, is a country of people with deep-rooted customs and religion. Respecting the culture will help you gain acceptance. Wear modest clothing upon entering any temple or religious site. Do not touch or attempt to shake hands with a monk, or touch anyone on the head. Always ask or signal a request before you take a close-up photo of someone, and wait for permission before you click the camera. The Myanmar New Year is celebrated in April with a four-day water festival. The religious ritual of gently pouring water over each other to wash away the bad sentiments of the previous year has evolved to include a fun-filled water game. The streets become crowded as young and old get involved, throwing water into passing cars, pouring water from upstairs windows onto pedestrians and cyclists, using whatever containers they can find. If you don't want to get wet, you have to stay indoors.

Tomato-Corn Chowder

This chowder is so good, so quick, and so easy. You can have supper ready in a flash by keeping these simple ingredients on hand.

INGREDIENTS SERVES 4–6

2 T.	margarine
2	large onions, chopped fine
1 c.	tomatoes, fresh or canned, chopped
2 c.	corn, canned
3 c.	creamed-style corn
1 can	evaporated milk

PREPARATION

1. Heat the margarine and sauté the onions until tender.
2. Add the tomatoes and simmer for 3 minutes.
3. Add the corn, creamed corn, and evaporated milk.
4. Stir until soup is hot, but not boiling.
5. Serve with crackers.

IF YOU GO TO NAMIBIA

During normal conversations, people usually stand about an arm's length away from each other. However, when lining up for something, such as boarding a bus or paying for purchases, it is common for folks to stand very close to one another. Men usually greet each other with a handshake, and women usually greet each other with words. If a woman wishes to show greater respect, a traditional greeting would include a handshake. At the same time, she would touch her own right elbow with her left hand, accompanied by a curtsy. Punctuality is not critical as it is generally accepted that you have shared time with others along the way. Weddings are extremely important social events in Namibia, often combining old and new traditions. For instance, vows may be said inside a church, but once outside, the guests might begin shouting, dancing, and waving horsetail whips.

Baby Spinach and Lentil Stew

A visit to the Himalayas in Nepal would be an absolute dream come true. With more than 1,300 peaks in the world's highest mountain range, it would be a sight to behold. Wherever we live, we can enjoy the view from our own windows while savoring this steaming stew. Ladle it over rice or scoop it up with thick bread.

INGREDIENTS SERVES 4–6

2 c.	lentils, soaked overnight in water
1 c.	vegetable stock
3 c.	milk
1 t.	turmeric
2	bay leaves
2 T.	oil
2	large onions, diced fine
2 c.	tomatoes, fresh or canned, chopped
3 cloves	garlic, minced
1 T.	fresh ginger, grated
1 t.	cumin
	salt to taste
1 lb.	baby spinach

PREPARATION

1. Drain and rinse the soaked lentils thoroughly.
2. Bring the stock and milk to a boil. Add the lentils, turmeric, bay leaves, and salt, if using. Reduce heat to low, cover, and simmer for 20 to 30 minutes or until the lentils are tender.
3. In a separate pan, heat the oil and fry the onions until translucent. Add the tomatoes, garlic, ginger, and cumin until heated through.
4. Combine with the lentils and vegetable stock and add the spinach. After the spinach wilts, add more vegetable stock or water if needed.

IF YOU GO TO NEPAL

One of the favorite pastimes of Nepali who live in rural areas is watching the foreign visitors who come to their country for mountain trekking. The children are especially interested in every move you make. Smile and enjoy their curiosity. Always remove your shoes before you enter any temple, and keep in mind that some temples are completely off limits to tourists. During meals, avoid licking your fingers. It is acceptable to make slurping sounds while sipping a hot drink. If you are sitting on the ground, it is impolite for someone to step over your legs, so if someone needs to get by, draw up your legs to enable that person to pass easily.

Creamy Brussels Sprouts Soup

This pretty soup is so smooth and creamy, no one would guess it is also low in fat. Served in pretty bowls, it would make a lovely addition to a holiday dinner, especially in the fall or winter. To ensure a mild flavor, take care not to overcook the Brussels sprouts. The Netherlands are one of the largest producers of Brussels sprouts in Europe. *In honor of Reinder and Aafje Bruinsma.*

INGREDIENTS **SERVES 4–6**

1 T.	olive oil
1	large onion, chopped
6 c.	vegetable stock
2	medium potatoes, peeled and diced
4 c.	fresh Brussels sprouts, trimmed
½ t.	salt
1 pinch	nutmeg
½ c.	milk

GARNISH

Fresh parsley or fresh dill

PREPARATION

1. In a large pan, cook the onion in the olive oil over low heat for 5 minutes.
2. Add the vegetable stock and potatoes. Bring to a boil. Reduce heat, cover, and simmer for 12 minutes.
3. Add the Brussels sprouts, salt, and nutmeg. Cook over low heat for 6 or 7 minutes, just until sprouts are cooked.
4. Puree the soup in a blender until smooth.
5. Return to pan and add the milk. Reheat gently; then serve.
6. Garnish with fresh parsley or fresh dill, if desired.

IF YOU GO TO THE NETHERLANDS

The Dutch tend to be practical people who value education, ambition, and hard work. They are careful with their money and find ostentatious behavior embarrassing. When meeting people, they will usually shake hands and say their last name. If no one is present to introduce you, introduce yourself. It is considered rude or suspicious not to identify yourself. In business matters, the Dutch may be the most experienced and successful traders in Europe. They tend to get right down to business and proceed with negotiations. You can take off your jacket during business meetings, but do not roll up your sleeves. Be sure to keep your hands out of your pockets while talking to someone. The Dutch are proud of their rich heritage of art, music, and involvement in international affairs.

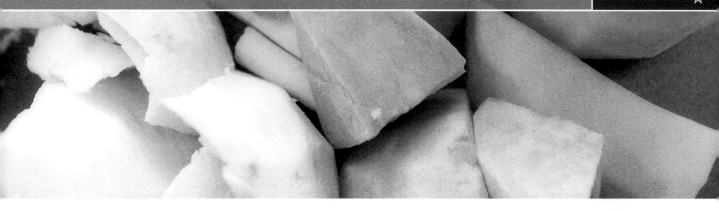

Sweet Potato–Parsnip Soup

Parsnips earn their due respect in this autumn-colored soup. If you love parsnips, add a couple more to the pot and adjust the liquid accordingly.

INGREDIENTS SERVES 6–8

2 T.	oil
2	large leeks, white part only
3	stalks celery, chopped
4 c.	sweet potatoes or yams, peeled and diced
2½ c.	parsnips, peeled and diced
1½ c.	potatoes, peeled and diced
4 c.	vegetable stock
2 c.	water
	salt to taste

GARNISH

Fresh parsley

PREPARATION

1. Heat the oil in a large saucepan. Add the leeks, celery, sweet potatoes, parsnips, and potatoes. Cook slowly over medium heat, stirring to prevent them from browning or sticking to the pan.
2. Stir in the vegetable stock and water and bring to a boil. Reduce the heat, cover, and simmer for 25 to 30 minutes or until vegetables are tender. Stir occasionally. Season to taste.
3. Puree in a blender until smooth. Return the soup to the rinsed pan and reheat slowly.
4. Ladle into soup bowls and garnish with sprigs of fresh parsley.

IF YOU GO TO NEW ZEALAND

New Zealanders goodnaturedly refer to themselves as "kiwis," named after the nocturnal kiwi bird that is a symbol of their country. New Zealanders are known for their courtesy, hospitality, and their quick willingness to offer assistance without being asked. Say "How do you do?" when you are introduced to someone, accompanied by a handshake and a smile. The country is also known for the rich Maori culture brought by settlers from Polynesia. The traditional Maori greeting involves people lightly rubbing noses. This is used mostly at formal Maori events, so don't try this with the general population on the street. In some areas, meals are baked in underground pits, cooked by thermal heat. New Zealand is well known for raising sheep that produce high-quality wool. It is also a hiker's paradise with trails winding around volcanoes and through lush forests.

Sweet Raisin and Rice Soup

Perfect for a light supper or a sweet ending to a fuller meal, this simple soup has been a sentimental favorite for many Scandinavians since childhood. Serve it warm; but if there is any left for tomorrow, serve it cold. *This recipe is in honor of Jan and Kari Paulsen.*

INGREDIENTS SERVES 4–6

6 c.	water
⅓ c.	rice
½ c.	raisins
1 stick	cinnamon
1 T.	flour
1 c.	heavy cream
¼ c.	sugar
¼ t.	salt

GARNISH

Cinnamon
Bananas, sliced

PREPARATION

1. In a heavy pan, combine the water, rice, raisins, and cinnamon stick. Bring to a boil. Reduce heat and simmer for 20 minutes, or until the rice is tender.

2. In a small bowl, whisk the flour into the cream. Stir the cream mixture into the soup.
3. Bring to a boil, then reduce heat and simmer for 2 minutes.
4. Stir in the sugar and salt. Remove the cinnamon stick and discard.
5. Serve hot or cold.

IF YOU GO TO NORWAY

Norway is filled with breathtaking natural beauty. Stunning views of mountains, fjords, lakes, mist, and forests are everywhere you look. The coastline is dotted with picturesque fishing villages that are so stirringly beautiful, you could be forgiven for thinking they were established for your benefit. Punctuality is very important in Norway. If you have an appointment, you should make every effort to be on time. Even if you are going to be only five minutes late, you should call your host out of respect and consideration. Cloudberries are highly prized in Norway. Be sure to try cloudberry jam on toast or ice cream while you are there.

Hummus, Tahini, and Pasta Soup √

This delicious soup doesn't take long to prepare. The taste and texture can be adjusted by adding more garbanzos or pasta, or it can be served over rice for a more substantial meal.

INGREDIENTS SERVES 6–8

1	15-oz. can garbanzos
½ t.	salt
2 cloves	garlic
¼ c.	tahini (pureed raw sesame seeds)
¼ c.	fresh lemon juice
4 c.	vegetable stock
1½ c.	pasta, uncooked

GARNISH
Chopped parsley or cilantro

PREPARATION

1. Puree the garbanzos, including the liquid from the can, salt, garlic, tahini, and lemon juice until smooth and creamy. (You may add some of the vegetable stock if it is too thick to blend until smooth.)
2. Bring the vegetable stock to a boil. Whisk in the hummus mixture. Simmer for 15 to 20 minutes.
3. Add the uncooked pasta. Simmer for 10 to 15 minutes until pasta is tender.
4. Ladle into bowls and garnish as desired. Serve with warm slices of pita bread.

IF YOU GO TO OMAN

Greetings from one man to another may be a kiss on the nose or on both cheeks, accompanied by a handshake. Women usually greet each other in much the same way. Men and women do not touch each other during greetings in public. You may be offered a small dish of dates as a gesture of hospitality. When interacting with Omanis, avoid confrontation; saving face is of utmost importance. Long periods of silence during conversations are to be expected and should not be interpreted as awkward. Oman is famous for its pink Mohammadi roses and its rosewater factories. The most intensive work in the rose business occurs during the five weeks of harvest. For the best results, roses are handpicked before dawn. For optimal scent and flavor, the distillation process begins the same morning they are picked. Rosewater is used in Arabic cooking, religious ceremonies, and in medicinal remedies for common ailments.

PAKISTAN

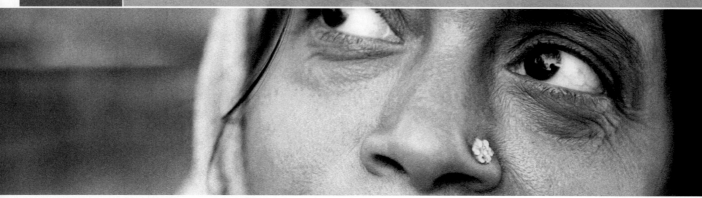

Spicy Cauliflower and Potato Stew

If you are worried about the degree of spiciness in this recipe, you can reduce the quantity of spices or just leave out the chili powder. The yogurt has a smooth, cooling effect, so you might want to try the stew as it is written below. This thick stew is especially good when it is served over rice.

INGREDIENTS SERVES 4–6

2 T.	oil
1 t.	mustard seeds
2 t.	cumin seeds
1 t.	ginger
½ t.	chili powder (add more as needed, or omit)
1	medium cauliflower, divided into small florets
3 c.	potatoes, boiled, peeled, and diced
1 c.	water
1½ c.	plain yogurt
	salt to taste

PREPARATION

1. Heat the oil in a large, heavy pan. When the oil is hot, add the mustard and cumin seeds and stir until they begin to pop. Then stir in the ginger and chili powder.
2. Add the cauliflower, potatoes, and water. Stir to mix evenly.
3. Cover and simmer for about 15 minutes, or until the cauliflower is still a bit crisp.
4. Stir in the yogurt and mix together well. Simmer for an additional 5 minutes or until hot. Do not let the mixture come to a boil.
5. Serve over rice.

IF YOU GO TO PAKISTAN

Pakistan is a country with an endless number of religious and secular festivals, fairs, and celebrations. Sporting events such as camel racing are highly competitive. Shoes are usually removed when entering a home. In rural areas, it is still common to eat meals from a knee-high table while sitting on the floor. You will be urged to take second and third helpings. Saying that you are too full will not be taken at face value, but merely accepted as a polite gesture. Eat only with your right hand. Business meetings start only after prolonged inquiries about health and family, although men should avoid asking direct questions about a colleague's wife or daughters.

PANAMA

Potato, Cheese, and Avocado Soup

Potatoes add an element of comfort and familiarity to most of the world's cuisine. You barely need to look at the recipe to make this lovely soup. Topped with avocados, the soup is filling and satisfying.

INGREDIENTS `SERVES 4–6`

2 T.	oil
1	large onion, chopped
7	large russet potatoes, peeled and diced
1½ t.	salt
6 c.	water
1½ c.	evaporated milk
1¼ c.	cheese, grated

GARNISH

2 or 3 avocados, sliced or diced

PREPARATION

1. Heat the oil in a large pan and sauté the onion until tender.
2. Add the potatoes and stir quickly to coat with oil and onions.
3. Add the salt and water and bring to a boil. Reduce heat and partially cover the pan so the potato water doesn't boil over. Simmer for 25 to 30 minutes or until the potatoes are very tender.
4. Use a potato masher to coarsely mash the potatoes in the pan. The soup does not need to be smooth, but it should be thick.
5. Add the milk and cheese, stirring constantly until the cheese is melted and the soup is heated through. Take care not to let the soup boil or stick to the bottom of the pan.
6. When ready to serve, ladle into individual bowls and top each bowl with sliced avocados.

IF YOU GO TO PANAMA

Look for sea turtles in the water along the coast of Panama, and make a point of getting up early to enjoy a Caribbean sunrise. Watch a few freighters traverse through the Panama Canal, and then make an effort to get out of the city to see parts of the rain forest. If all goes well, you'll spot a few capuchin monkeys, and you might get to meet indigenous people selling handmade items at the market. Viewing the sunset over the Pacific Ocean might be the perfect end to a wonderful day.

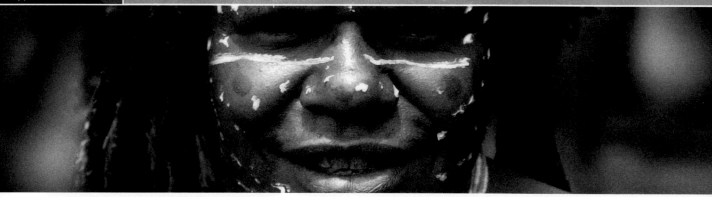

Sweet Potato and Red Lentil Soup

More sweet potatoes are consumed per capita in Papua New Guinea than in any other country of the world. They are readily available in the highland areas.

INGREDIENTS SERVES 4–6

3 T.	olive oil
2 t.	curry powder
2	medium onions, grated
2	medium apples, peeled, cored, and grated
3	medium sweet potatoes or yams, peeled and diced
3 cloves	garlic, crushed
3 T.	cilantro, chopped
1-inch piece	ginger, peeled and grated fine
5 c.	water
1 c.	red lentils
1½ t.	fresh lime juice

PREPARATION

1. In a large, heavy pan, combine the oil, curry powder, onions, and apples. Stir and cook for about 10 minutes, or until the onions are translucent.

2. Stir in the sweet potatoes, garlic, cilantro, ginger, water, and red lentils. Bring to a boil; then reduce heat to medium low. Cover and simmer the lentils and vegetables for 30 minutes, or until the lentils and vegetables are tender. Add the lime juice and stir.

3. Place one-third or half of the ingredients in a blender. Blend until smooth. Repeat until all the ingredients have been blended.

4. Return to the pan and reheat. Add more water if needed.

5. Serve hot.

IF YOU GO TO PAPUA NEW GUINEA

More than 800 languages are spoken in this country. Most adults are able to speak at least three languages. Volcanoes and rugged terrain make it challenging to travel in Papua New Guinea. For a good look around, you might want to consider a tour in a small plane. Check out the rain forest habitat in Lae and look for tree kangaroos and turtles.

Zucchini-Rice Soup

This soup can be made with zucchini or yellow crookneck squash, or some of both. Either way, it tastes like summer.

INGREDIENTS `SERVES 4–6`

1 T.	oil
1	medium onion, chopped fine
2 cloves	garlic
4 c.	vegetable stock
2 c.	water
¼ c.	white rice, uncooked
2	medium zucchini, unpeeled and grated
¼ t.	salt
¼ c.	parmesan cheese

PREPARATION

1. In a large pan, heat the oil and sauté the onion and garlic until tender.
2. Add the stock and water and bring to a boil.
3. Add the rice and cook on low for 10 minutes.
4. Add the grated zucchini and salt.
5. Simmer on low, partially covered, for 15 minutes.
6. Add the parmesan cheese while stirring the mixture.
7. Let the soup simmer for 2 minutes before serving.

IF YOU GO TO PARAGUAY

Paraguayans value tranquility, friendship, and good manners. Personal relationships are considered more valuable than business relationships, so it is essential to take time for small talk, especially if you are planning to do business in Paraguay. It is customary for men and women to shake hands, even if they have met earlier in the day. Gifts from your home country or region are appreciated. Dinner is rarely served before 9:00 P.M. If you decide to host a dinner in Paraguay, 7:00 P.M. would be far too early. Invite people at 8:30 or 9:00 P.M., and expect to serve dinner by 10:00 P.M. Even if you are entertaining business contacts, dinner is purely a social event. Do not discuss business at the table unless your most senior guest initiates it.

Polka-Dot Potato Soup

Small chopped vegetables add a colorful polka-dot appearance to this warm and wonderful potato soup. Some families enjoy this soup on Christmas Eve, but the rest of us can enjoy it any time of the year.

INGREDIENTS SERVES 6-8

3 T.	margarine
2	leeks, white part only, chopped
2 cloves	garlic, minced
3 T.	flour
3	large carrots, chopped
3	stalks celery, chopped
1	medium red bell pepper, chopped
4 c.	corn, canned
6 c.	low-fat milk
4	large potatoes, peeled and diced
1½ c.	peas, frozen and thawed
½ c.	fresh basil, chopped
	salt to taste

PREPARATION

1. In a large pan, heat the margarine and sauté the leeks and garlic until soft.
2. Add the flour, stirring quickly to coat the leeks and garlic, and cook for 3 minutes
3. Add the carrots, celery, bell pepper, and corn.
4. Slowly add the milk, stirring constantly. Cook carefully for 6 to 8 minutes. Do not allow the milk to boil at any time during the process.
5. Add the potatoes and cook until tender.
6. Add the peas and stir in the chopped basil. Serve warm.

IF YOU GO TO PERU

Most people who visit Peru make a point of visiting Machu Picchu, the ancient ruins perched high in the Andes. Another popular place is Lake Titicaca, the world's highest commercially navigable lake, located 12,500 feet above sea level. Photo opportunities of this rugged country are endless. Be respectful around religious buildings—in some cases, photos are prohibited. The vibrant colors of the regional dress and gala folk festivals are hugely popular with visitors. This is tourism at the local level, so you may be expected to tip for photos.

Tofu-Corn Soup

Some versions of corn soup have a thinner consistency than this particular recipe, but you can simply adjust the liquid according to your taste. And if you like spicy soup, throw in a hot pepper. *In honor of Nimfa Sumagaysay and Jemima Orilloso.*

INGREDIENTS — SERVES 4–6

1 T.	oil
1	medium block of tofu, diced
2 cloves	garlic, minced
½ t.	fresh ginger, grated
4	medium green onions, white and green parts, sliced diagonally
4 c.	water
1½ c.	coconut milk
3 c.	creamed-style corn
1½ T.	soy sauce
2 c.	watercress or spinach, chopped

PREPARATION

1. Heat the oil and stir-fry the tofu until light brown.
2. Stir in the garlic, ginger, and green onions and fry for 2 minutes, stirring frequently.
3. Add the water, coconut milk, creamed corn, and soy sauce. Cover and simmer for 10 minutes.
4. Add the watercress or spinach and cook for 2 or 3 minutes or until the greens have wilted.
5. Adjust the liquid if needed, and serve.

IF YOU GO TO THE PHILIPPINES

If you are a guest in someone's home in the Philippines, it would be a thoughtful gesture to take a small gift of sweets for the hosts. However, it is not a good idea to take a fruit basket because it could be perceived that you don't think they can provide adequately for you. The typical eating utensils are a fork and soupspoon. Meals are usually served family style or buffet style. Do not help yourself to any of the food until you have been urged several times. Folks in the Philippines tend to be very friendly, outgoing, and happy. They are exceedingly generous hosts. If you are presented with a business card, be sure to receive it with both hands. You should examine it briefly before putting it away.

Blueberry Summer Soup

This delightful chilled soup can be served as an appetizer, a dessert soup, or a light meal when served with muffins or scones. While you are enjoying the taste and texture, imagine relaxing beside one of the beautiful lakes in Poland. *Shared by my friend Frances Olsey.*

INGREDIENTS SERVES 4–6

⅓ c.	sugar
½ c.	water
4 c.	blueberries, fresh or frozen (thawed if frozen)
½ c.	apple juice
1 c.	sour cream, light or regular

GARNISH

Whipped cream, any kind

PREPARATION

1. Combine the sugar and water in a medium saucepan over medium-high heat.
2. Stir in the blueberries.
3. Cook until the blueberries pop and become soft, stirring frequently.
4. Strain the blueberries and save the liquid in a large bowl.
5. Use a potato masher to break down the fruit. Press the pulp through a sieve. Either discard the remaining pulp, or add it to the liquid.
6. Stir the apple juice into the liquid.
7. Stir in the sour cream until fully blended and smooth.
8. Serve cold, topped with whipped cream.

IF YOU GO TO POLAND

Conservative dress is greatly appreciated in Poland, so leave your sweatpants at home. The culture may seem more formal than you expected, but Poles are very friendly and polite. Be sure to greet people upon entering or exiting an elevator. Smile and maintain eye contact when shaking hands. Respect the culture and history, but refrain from bringing up sensitive topics such as politics and past wars. If possible, visit the Church of Peace in Jawor or the Church of Peace in Swidnica. Both are listed as World Heritage sites due to the age and history of their timber structures. The composer Frederic Chopin was born near Warsaw.

Mediterranean Red Bell Pepper Soup

Red bell peppers bring bright color and robust flavor to Mediterranean cooking. This exceptional soup is packed with both elements. It tastes even better when served with warm olive bread.

INGREDIENTS SERVES 4–6

2	red bell peppers, sliced (seeds removed)
1	onion, sliced
2 cloves	garlic, minced
1	green chili, chopped (seeds removed)
3 c.	diced tomatoes with juice (or 1 28-oz. can)
3 c.	vegetable bouillon or stock
2 T.	fresh basil, chopped
	salt to taste

GARNISH, OPTIONAL

Additional sprigs of basil or cubed bread may be used to garnish each bowl of soup

PREPARATION

1. Put the red bell peppers, onion, garlic, and chili in a large, heavy pan. Add the tomatoes and bouillon or stock and bring to a boil over medium heat, stirring frequently.
2. Reduce heat to low and simmer for 30 minutes or until the bell peppers are tender.
3. Drain, saving the liquid in a separate pan.
4. Puree the vegetables by pressing through a strainer with the back of a spoon, or process in a blender until smooth.
5. Combine the puree with the reserved cooking liquid. Add the basil and heat until hot.

IF YOU GO TO PORTUGAL

Lisbon, the capital of Portugal, is a city filled with spectacular views and photo opportunities. In the Old Quarter, the Alfama neighborhood is a winding, confusing maze of streets so narrow, few cars can navigate through it. You'll see laundry flapping from clotheslines above the walkways, canaries in birdcages on balconies, and flower pots in windowsills. With all of the archways and flights of stairs, there is much to see. During the summer, the streets are even more crowded as visitors walk through the neighborhood, enjoying a close-up view of life in this preserved area of Portugal.

Tomato-Vegetable Soup

With this big batch of tomato-vegetable soup, you'll have enough soup to share with the neighbors, or you can take it easy tomorrow by enjoying it a second time. Its versatility allows you to mix and match vegetables as you wish.

INGREDIENTS SERVES 8–10

5 c.	water
3 c.	tomato sauce, canned
1 c.	tomato paste
3	medium potatoes, diced
3	medium carrots, sliced thin
1	large onion, chopped
2 cloves	garlic, minced
2	medium celery stalks, sliced thin
¼ c.	Italian parsley, chopped fine
1 c.	fresh green beans, sliced into 1-inch pieces
¼ t.	cumin
⅛ t.	ginger
⅛ t.	cinnamon
1 t.	salt
½ c.	small pasta shells

PREPARATION

1. In a large pan, whisk the water, tomato sauce, and tomato paste until smooth.
2. Add the remaining vegetables and spices. Bring to a boil, then reduce heat and simmer for 30 minutes.
3. Add the pasta shells and cook for 15 more minutes or until pasta and vegetables are tender. Add more water if needed.

IF YOU GO TO QATAR

Learn to say *"Salaam"* in Qatar, and people will appreciate your friendly hello. Check out the futuristic architecture in Doha and the timeless beauty of old mosques in Al-Wakrah. Desert excursions are popular with visitors, as well as trips to view ancient rock carvings. Fruit juices are widely available here. While in Qatar, make a point of trying yogurt made from goat's milk.

Apple Orchard Soup

The scent of apples and cinnamon never fails to wake up your sentimental side. Relax and enjoy this fragrant soup.

INGREDIENTS SERVES 4–6

5	medium apples, peeled and cut into chunks
8 c.	water
2 T.	sugar
1 T.	fresh lemon juice
1 t.	cinnamon
2 T.	cornstarch
½ c.	apple juice
1 c.	light cream

PREPARATION

1. Bring the apples and water to a boil.
2. Stir in the sugar, lemon juice, and cinnamon. Reduce heat, cover, and simmer for 20 minutes or until the apples are very soft.
3. In a small bowl, whisk the cornstarch into the apple juice until smooth. Stir into the apple mixture, stirring constantly, until thickened.
4. Stir in the cream and set aside for a few minutes before serving.

IF YOU GO TO ROMANIA

Romanians tend to be formal and reserved in their interactions with each other. Respect for privacy is highly valued. They are kind and polite, but they take their time when it comes to building relationships. Older men may kiss the hand of a woman in greeting, but foreign men are not expected to do so. At mealtimes, keep your hands visible at all times. You may rest your wrists on the edge of the table, but do not put your hands in your lap. You will be repeatedly offered second and third helpings even though you may insist that you cannot eat any more. It is acceptable to soak up extra sauce or gravy with your bread.

Mushroom-Barley Soup

One can only guess how many versions of mushroom-barley soup exist. Barley adds substance to soup that seems to contribute to a sense of satisfaction and contentment after the first bowl. *This recipe is in honor of Mikhail and Lyudmila Kulakov.*

INGREDIENTS SERVES 8–10

3 T.	margarine or butter
4 c.	white mushrooms, sliced
2	medium leeks, white part only, halved and sliced
1	large onion, chopped
3 T.	parsley, chopped
4½ c.	water
2 or 3	bouillon cubes
½ c.	barley, uncooked
3	medium carrots, peeled and diced
2	stalks celery, diced
2 c.	milk
½ t.	salt

PREPARATION

1. In a medium pan, melt the margarine and sauté the mushrooms, leeks, and onion for 5 to 8 minutes or until tender. Add the parsley and set aside.
2. In a large, heavy pan, bring the water, bouillon cubes, and barley to a boil.
3. Add the carrots and celery and bring back to a boil. Reduce heat, cover, and simmer for about 45 minutes, or until the barley is tender.
4. Add the mushroom mixture and milk. Heat thoroughly.
5. Season with salt and serve.

Note: If you prefer a thicker soup, combine ½ c. of the milk while it is still cold with ¼ c. of flour. Gradually stir into soup. Bring to a low boil, reduce heat, and simmer for 5 minutes or until thickened.

IF YOU GO TO RUSSIA

Russian culture is defined by the way people relate to their families. Great respect is given to *babushkas*, the elderly matriarchs who usually live with their children and often provide child care for the younger generations. If you visit a Russian home, it is almost mandatory that you bring a gift. They may protest when it is offered, but that is part of the protocol before it is accepted. Smiles are reserved for things that they find amusing or when greeting close friends. Smiling at strangers in public is considered suspicious.

Lentil-Zucchini Soup

This thick soup is hearty enough to make a satisfying meal. Many variations of this savory soup have been served to pilgrims on their journey to Mecca. Fresh lemons make this recipe special.

INGREDIENTS `SERVES 8–10`

8 c.	water
1½ c.	dried lentils
1	medium onion, chopped fine
3 or 4 cloves	garlic, minced
1	large potato, peeled and diced
2	stalks celery, chopped fine
2	medium zucchini, peeled and diced
¾ t.	cumin
1 t.	salt

GARNISH

2 lemons, cut into wedges, to serve on the side

PREPARATION

1. Place the lentils, onion, and garlic in a large stockpot and cover with water. Bring to a boil, then reduce heat and simmer, covered, for 20 minutes.
2. Add the potatoes and celery. Cook, covered, for 15 minutes.
3. Add the zucchini, cumin, and salt. Continued to cook for another 15 minutes, or until the potatoes and lentils are tender.
4. When ready to serve, ladle the soup into bowls. Sprinkle each with a dash of fresh lemon juice. Serve a lemon wedge with each portion.

IF YOU GO TO SAUDI ARABIA

Saudi Arabia is home to Mecca, the holiest city in Islam. It is the goal of millions of Muslims to make at least one pilgrimage to Mecca during their lifetime. Men greet each other with a handshake, an embrace, and possibly one to three kisses on alternating cheeks. Women might also kiss each other one to three times, such as once on the right cheek and twice on the left. Men and women rarely touch each other in public. When seated, avoid crossing your legs or showing the bottom of your feet or shoes. It is the usual custom to remove your shoes upon entering a carpeted room. Women should wear loose clothing and take care not to expose collarbones or knees. Saudis have a fine reputation for generous hospitality, showering their guests with an abundance of food. Conversation during meals is minimal so that everyone can fully enjoy each item that is served.

Scottish Broth

Don't be fooled into thinking Scottish Broth is something to sip from a teacup. It is actually a very hearty soup, sometimes described as "evening porridge" because it is a meal in itself. The vegetables can be interchanged; but to be Scottish broth, the soup must contain barley. This soup tastes even better on the second day.

INGREDIENTS SERVES 4–6

½ c.	pearl barley
2 T.	margarine
2	medium onions, chopped
8 c.	water
5	medium carrots, chopped
4	stalks celery, chopped
2	medium turnips, peeled and diced
¼ t.	rosemary
1 t.	salt

PREPARATION

1. In a medium bowl, cover the barley with boiling water. Cover the bowl with a plate while you prepare the vegetables.
2. Melt the margarine in a large pan. Cook the onions for 5 minutes.
3. Add the water, carrots, celery, turnips, rosemary, and salt. Drain the barley and add it to the vegetables. Bring to a boil, then cover and reduce heat. Simmer for about 45 minutes or until the vegetables and barley are tender.

IF YOU GO TO SCOTLAND

In order to blend in with the folks in Scotland, mind your manners when it comes to drinking tea. There are a few dos and don'ts to keep in mind. Do fill your cup three-quarters full or slightly less. This will help to prevent spills when you lift the cup. Don't cradle the teacup in your hands if it has a handle. Do place your spoon on the saucer; never leave it standing upright in the cup. When you stir, take care not to make unnecessary noise. Stirring should be gentle and silent, never hitting the sides of the cup with your spoon. Now you can sit back, relax, and be part of the local culture.

Regal Cream Soup With Cherry Tomatoes

This creamy, rich soup with undertones of curry should be served very cold. Just before serving, add fresh cherry tomatoes, sliced into rounds. Senegal is one of the world's largest exporters of cherry tomatoes. This makes an elegant appetizer or first course soup. *This recipe is in honor of Ganoune Diop.*

INGREDIENTS SERVES 4–6

2 T.	margarine
2 T.	finely diced onions
2 t.	curry powder
3 T.	flour
4 c.	vegetable stock
2 c.	heavy cream
1 c.	cherry tomatoes, slice into rounds

PREPARATION

1. Melt the margarine in a large pan and sauté the onions until they are translucent.
2. Add the curry and flour and quickly stir to coat the onions.
3. Add the vegetable stock a little at a time, whisking until smooth.
4. Bring to a boil and cook for 1 minute. Strain the soup to remove the onions and any lumps. Let the soup cool for one hour. Stir in the cream and refrigerate until completely chilled. May be made a day ahead if desired. The soup should be served cold.

5. Just before serving, add the cherry tomatoes. Garnish each serving with one thin slice of cherry tomato if desired.

VARIATIONS

- Other vegetables could be substituted for the cherry tomatoes.
- Leave out cherry tomatoes and serve as a smooth soup in tiny teacups.

IF YOU GO TO SENEGAL

While in Senegal, dress modestly and be aware that in some areas men and women may be seated at separate tables or in different rooms. You may compliment your hosts on artwork or articles in their home, but don't overdo it. The Senegalese are generous people and may feel obliged to give them to you. Refusing to accept a gift may offend your host, so it is wise to be thoughtful and as well-mannered as possible. Conversations may be filled with metaphors and stories to illustrate points.

Raspberry Soup

Keep frozen fruit on hand in the freezer for quick and colorful soups and desserts. Try this Old World recipe and use your imagination and experiment with other frozen fruit. Serbia grows up to one-third of all the raspberries in the world and is the leading exporters of this beloved fruit. *This recipe is in memory of my brother-in-law John Jeider.*

INGREDIENTS SERVES 4–6

3 c.	raspberries, frozen and thawed (reserve 12 raspberries for garnish)
4 c.	water
¾ c.	sugar (sugar may be reduced if you don't use lemon juice)
1 t.	fresh lemon juice
4 T.	tapioca
1 t.	vanilla
½ t.	lemon zest

PREPARATION

1. In a medium saucepan, add the raspberries, water, sugar, and lemon juice and bring to a boil. Cook until sugar is completely dissolved.
2. Strain the soup to remove the seeds, or press through a sieve. (If you don't mind the seeds, you can skip this step.)
3. Return the mixture to the stove over medium heat. Add the tapioca and vanilla. Cook until thickened.
4. When ready to serve, ladle into bowls and top with reserved raspberries and lemon zest.
5. May serve either hot or cold.

VARIATIONS

- Carefully float fresh fruit on top, such as bananas, or paper-thin slices of kiwi or nectarines.
- Serve over a scoop of frozen yogurt or ice cream.

IF YOU GO TO SERBIA

Serbians tend to be industrious, earnest in their Orthodox faith, and appreciative of folklore and intellectual thought. They are quietly hospitable, quick to throw a rug on the ground beside a lake, roadside, or an orchard for a picnic. Long discussions of philosophy may ensue. Serbians typically have three meals each day. Breakfast gives the day a hearty start, lunch is the main meal, usually taken around 3:00 P.M., and a light supper may be served around 8:00 P.M. It is customary for several generations to live together under the same roof, and the household may include cousins, aunts, and uncles.

SINGAPORE

Orange-Ginger-Carrot Soup

Show off this bright orange soup in clear glass bowls or teacups. A colorful, gingery choice for a first course or as an appetizer served in small cups. *In honor of my friends from Far Eastern Academy, especially the class of '72.*

INGREDIENTS SERVES 4–6

1½ T.	peanut or other oil
4	medium carrots, sliced thin
2	medium leeks, white part only, sliced
1 T.	fresh ginger, grated
2½ c.	vegetable stock or water
2 c.	orange juice
pinch	salt

GARNISH

2 medium green onions, sliced

PREPARATION

1. Heat the oil and sauté the carrots, leeks, and ginger for 8 minutes, stirring frequently.
2. Add the vegetable stock or water and bring to a boil. Reduce heat, cover, and simmer for 20 minutes or until the carrots are tender.
3. Puree the soup in a food processor or blender until smooth.
4. Add the orange juice.
5. Let the mixture cool for 20 minutes; then refrigerate until thoroughly chilled.
6. Garnish with sliced green onions and serve.

IF YOU GO TO SINGAPORE

A thoroughly modern island country, Singapore has made the most of its deep harbors and strategic location. It is one of the busiest shipping ports in the world and is well known for international trade and tourism. Many cultures converge in the workplace, but ethnic and religious groups maintain their own identity through festivals and celebrations. Singapore is admired for its well-placed flower gardens. You'll find tropical flowers on roundabouts, street corners, hotel rooftops, and in residential areas. English is readily spoken and understood, making it easy to get around the island for shopping and sightseeing.

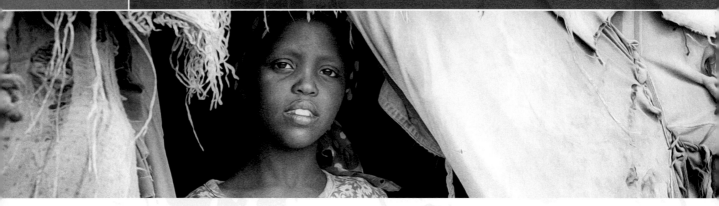

Mild Curried Corn Soup

These ingredients are easy to keep on hand. The curry is mild and adds a lovely flavor to the corn and tomatoes. Serve this stew and you can expect compliments.

INGREDIENTS   SERVES 4–6

1 T.	margarine
1	medium onion, chopped coarse
2 cloves	garlic
½ t.	curry powder
5 c.	corn, fresh or frozen
1 t.	cornstarch
1⅔ c.	coconut milk
2 c.	tomatoes, fresh or canned, chopped coarse
½ t.	salt

PREPARATION

1. In a large pan, melt the margarine and add the onion and garlic. Cook until lightly browned.
2. Add the curry powder, stirring quickly to coat the onion. Add the corn and stir, continuing to cook.
3. Place the cornstarch in a bowl and slowly add the coconut milk, whisking quickly to prevent lumps. Add this to the corn mixture and stir well.
4. Add the tomatoes and salt. Cook over low heat for about 7 minutes, stirring occasionally. The coconut milk should be mostly absorbed. If you prefer a thinner consistency, add water or milk, a little at a time.
5. Serve warm.

IF YOU GO TO SOMALIA

Looking for something different to do? A trip to a livestock market might be worth a visit. Observe the haggling, take photos only with permission, and make sure you don't inadvertently buy a camel. Expect to be watched by people who are simply intrigued and curious about you. Some reefs around the islands just off the shore of Somalia are reported to have a wealth of aquatic life.

Butternut Squash Soup

Butternut squash is so plentiful throughout South Africa that farm stands sell them in sacks of 15 or so. Often referred to as pumpkins, the squash is typically curried or scented with sweet spices. This outstanding soup has a surprise ingredient—a roasted banana. But you can leave it out if you prefer. *This recipe is in honor of Dr. Peter and Ros Landless.*

INGREDIENTS SERVES 4–6

4 c.	butternut squash, peeled and diced
2 T.	brown sugar
2 T.	honey
4 T.	oil, divided
1	medium ripe banana
1	small onion, chopped
2	medium carrots, chopped
2	stalks celery, chopped
2 cloves	garlic, minced
1 t.	curry powder
½ t.	coriander
¼ t.	nutmeg
1 c.	coconut milk
1 c.	water
2 t.	fresh lime juice
1 t.	salt

PREPARATION

1. Preheat the oven to 350°F. Place the squash in a baking pan, then sprinkle with brown sugar, honey, and 2 T. of oil. Bake the unpeeled banana in the same pan with the squash. Roast until the squash is caramelized and soft, about 20 minutes.
2. In a large pan, add 2 T. of oil and sauté the onion, carrots, and celery until tender.
3. Add the spices and cook for 2 minutes, stirring frequently.
4. Remove the banana from its peel, slice it, and add it to the pan. Add the squash, coconut milk, and water. Simmer until hot.
5. Transfer to a blender and process until smooth. Add the lime juice and salt. Reheat if necessary, and serve.

IF YOU GO TO SOUTH AFRICA

South Africa is a kaleidoscope of cultures, diverse landscapes, and astounding wildlife. Tourists flock to the game parks or stop to observe migrating whales along the coast. Safari etiquette dictates that you not imitate animal sounds or try to corner a wild animal. Be on the safe side and heed the advice of the safari guide. Be aware that you could also encounter wild animals outside of game parks.

Gazpacho Rico

Gazpacho is a traditional peasant soup made from fresh tomatoes and bell peppers, plus any other available fresh vegetables. At the end of a hard day in the factory or field, workers would look forward to cooling off with this *rico* (tasty) chilled tomato soup. Serve it with crusty bread and a side dish of your favorite olives. *In honor of my nephew Benjamin Child, who gave this recipe its name.*

INGREDIENTS SERVES 4–6

6	ripe tomatoes, peeled and chopped
1	onion, chopped fine
1	cucumber, peeled and seeded, chopped
1	red or green bell pepper, seeded, chopped
2	stalks celery, chopped
2 T.	parsley or cilantro
1 clove	garlic, minced
½ c.	olive oil
2 T.	fresh lemon juice
1 T.	sugar
4 c.	tomato juice

PREPARATION

1. Combine all the ingredients in a large bowl. Blend in small batches, just until desired consistency is achieved.

2. Store it in the refrigerator in a nonmetal container. Chill thoroughly and allow flavors to blend.

IF YOU GO TO SPAIN

Spain is the world's leading producer of olives and grows the widest variety. During the seventeenth century, olives were served as a dessert rather than as an appetizer or side dish. When dining at someone's home or at a restaurant, plates of olives will appear at the table almost immediately. Bread and butter plates are not used because bread is typically set directly on the table. Utensils are used for most food, even for fruit. Mealtimes are highly social activities and are considered vital to maintaining relationships. Expect to be interrupted when speaking. In most villages or big cities, churches and cathedrals tend to be ornate. Some are now museums and are open to visitors.

SRI LANKA

Curried Lentil Stew

Add this delicious curry to your repertoire of lentil recipes. The secret to this savory stew is the coconut milk and the aromatic spices. *This recipe is in honor of P. Perumal Dhanaraja.*

INGREDIENTS SERVES 4–6

1 c.	lentils, uncooked
1 T.	oil
1	medium onion, diced
2 cloves	garlic, minced
1 t.	curry powder
1 t.	chili powder (add more if you like it spicy hot)
½ t.	coriander
2 c.	coconut milk
2 c.	milk
	salt to taste

PREPARATION

1. Wash and soak the lentils in water for at least 1 hour.
2. In a large pan, heat the oil and sauté the onion, garlic, and curry powder until onion is soft.
3. Rinse and drain the lentils and add to the pan.
4. Add the chili powder, coriander, coconut milk, and milk.
5. Bring to a boil, then simmer on low until lentils are soft. Add salt to taste.
6. Serve alone or over rice.

IF YOU GO TO SRI LANKA

If you are invited to dinner at a specified time, you should plan to be on time even though it may be several hours before the food arrives. (You might need to eat something before you go.) Since most of the socializing takes place before the meal is served, you can expect to leave within half an hour after the meal ends. While in Sri Lanka, plan to visit the Pinnawela Elephant Orphanage near Kegalle. Originally established to care for injured or orphaned elephants found in the wild, it is now home to about 70 elephants. If you visit during feeding time, you can offer sugar cane and bananas to the calves. You can also accompany the entire herd to the nearby river and watch the elephants enjoy their daily baths.

SWEDEN

Winter Fruit Soup

For many Scandinavians, fruit soup is a winter tradition, especially on Christmas Eve. It may be served as a light meal, enjoyed as a dessert, ladled over toast, or even poured over ice cream. The taste and color varies according to the variety of fruits that are used. *This recipe is in honor of my Swedish grandmothers, Laura Davis and Eleanor Lyon.*

INGREDIENTS `SERVES 6–8`

1¾ c.	dried mixed fruit, chopped
½ c.	dried cranberries
1	cinnamon stick
3 T.	rice
4 c.	water
2¼ c.	orange juice
½ c.	lingonberry or cherry jam
¼ c.	sugar

PREPARATION

1. Combine the dried fruit, dried cranberries, cinnamon stick, rice, and water in a large pot. Bring to a boil, then reduce heat and simmer uncovered for 30 minutes.
2. Stir in the orange juice, jam, and sugar. Bring to a boil, then reduce heat and simmer covered for 15 minutes. Stir occasionally to keep contents from sticking.
3. Serve warm.

IF YOU GO TO SWEDEN

Swedes are patriotic and tend to be very proud of their nation, towns, and region. Do not praise one area in Sweden over the area you are currently visiting, as this would be considered impolite. It is more common for guests to be invited to a Swede's home for dessert than for a full meal. Punctuality is extremely important. If necessary, park your car around the corner and wait until you can arrive at the exact moment of the specified time. The most popular souvenir from Sweden is the wooden hand-painted Dala horse. Originally, Swedes living in small log cabins deep in the forests would whittle small toys from wood scraps. Because horses were invaluable to the work on farms and in the forests, it was only natural that so many horse carvings were made. Today, the Dala horse is a national symbol.

Barley Knob Soup

Would you know a knob of celeriac if you saw one? You might know it as a celery bulb. Celeriac has a muddy appearance on the outside, similar to a jicama and is about the size of an average rutabaga. Trim away the peelings and you'll discover a root vegetable that tastes like celery, but has no strings. If you've never tried celeriac before, you'll wonder why you waited so long.

INGREDIENTS SERVES 4–6

½ c.	barley
2 c.	boiling water
2 T.	oil
1 knob	celeriac (also called celery bulb), diced
2	medium carrots, diced
2	medium potatoes, peeled and diced
4 c.	cabbage, chopped (discard thick ribs)
2	leeks, sliced into rings
4 c.	vegetable stock
3 c.	water
¾ t.	salt

PREPARATION

1. Cover the barley with the boiling water and set aside for 30 minutes.
2. In a large, heavy pan, heat the oil and cook the celeriac, carrots, and potatoes for 8 minutes, stirring frequently.
3. Add the cabbage, leeks, vegetable stock, water, and salt.
4. Drain the barley and add to the soup. Simmer for 45 minutes.

IF YOU GO TO SWITZERLAND

Once you leave the cities, you are bound to see herds of the Brown Swiss cow. Known for their size and their superior cream, these cows are highly prized. Listen for the charming sound of cow bells as they graze, but you'll also hear the bells worn by sheep and goats. The Swiss are very proud of their promotion of worldwide peace. They also take pride in protecting the environment and keeping things neat and clean. If you litter, you can expect a public scolding. When dining, break bread with your hands instead of using a knife. If you don't see salt on the table, do not ask for it. Watch for the numerous waterfalls fed by melting mountain snow in the spring.

SYRIA

Lemon, Lentil, and Bulgur Soup

This soup is so nutritious and flavorful from the fresh mint and lemons, that you'll be planning to make a second batch soon.

INGREDIENTS `SERVES 6–8`

1 c.	bulgur
8 c.	vegetable stock
1 c.	lentils
¼ c.	flour
1 t.	salt
½ t.	cinnamon
¼ c.	green onion, chopped
¼ c.	fresh mint, chopped
¼ c.	parsley, chopped
2	lemons, juiced
3 or 4 cloves	garlic, minced
2 T.	olive oil

GARNISH

Yogurt or sour cream

PREPARATION

1. In a small bowl, cover the bulgur with water and soak for 30 minutes.
2. In a large stockpot, bring the vegetable stock and lentils to a boil for 10 minutes.
3. Reduce heat and simmer for 20 to 25 minutes or until the lentils are tender.
4. Drain the water from the soaked bulgur.
5. Add the flour, salt, cinnamon, green onion, mint, and parsley to the bulgur mixture. Stir until the ingredients are combined and the mixture is crumbly.
6. Add to the vegetable stock and lentils, simmering for 5 minutes.
7. Add the lemon juice, garlic, and oil. Simmer for 10 minutes.
8. Serve hot. Pita bread would make a nice accompaniment.

IF YOU GO TO SYRIA

Men and women usually socialize separately except in instances when the entire family is involved. Syrian cuisine is noted for its excellence in flavor and variety. Hospitality is often accompanied by mint tea. In the marketplace, you might have a chance to witness elaborate showmanship as tea vendors use flourishing motions to serve tea to customers. It has been said that the bazaar in Aleppo is one of the world's most unusual, due to its setting under vaulted ceilings.

Chinese Noodle Soup

Soup isn't reserved for lunch or dinner in Taiwan. It's often served for breakfast. Why not? With noodle soup this good, you won't mind either starting or finishing the day this way. *This recipe is in honor of Dr. Samuel Wang.*

INGREDIENTS `SERVES 4–6`

6 c.	vegetable stock
2 c.	sliced mushrooms (white, wood ear, or shiitake)
1	small can bamboo shoots
1	small can water chestnuts, sliced or chopped
6 to 8	medium green onions, white and light green parts only, sliced
3 cloves	garlic, minced
1	package lo mein noodles (or other Chinese noodles)
1 t.	chili oil (add more if desired)
2 T.	soy sauce
2 T.	rice vinegar (or 1 T. lemon or lime juice)

PREPARATION

1. In a large pan, bring the vegetable stock to a boil. Add the mushrooms, bamboo shoots, and water chestnuts. Reduce heat and simmer for 15 minutes.

2. Add the green onions, garlic, and noodles. Cook for 5 minutes; then stir in the chili oil.

3. Add the soy sauce, rice vinegar or lemon or lime juice, and simmer until the noodles are tender.

4. Taste and add more chili oil if desired.

IF YOU GO TO TAIWAN

The question "Have you eaten?" is a standard greeting in Taiwan, similar to "How are you?" in other countries. It's more of a rhetorical question. Good topics during dinner include art, family, and sightseeing. Always be polite and complimentary when you make comments about the local food, scenery, hotels, and sightseeing. Modesty is a great virtue here. If someone gives you a compliment, do not say, "Thank you." You will be received in much higher esteem if you insist that you do not deserve the compliment. Avoid touching anyone on the shoulder or head, and do not ever wink at anyone. Give and receive gifts with both hands.

TANZANIA

Golden Bean and Coconut Stew

The coconut milk adds such a smooth and delicious taste that you'll quickly make a point of keeping cans of coconut milk in your pantry at all times.

INGREDIENTS SERVES 6–8

2 c.	white beans, garbanzos, or other dried beans
1⅔ c.	coconut milk
2	small tomatoes, diced
3 cloves	garlic, minced
1½ t.	turmeric
½ t.	salt

PREPARATION

1. Soaks beans overnight. (You can use almost any kind of dried beans for this stew.) Rinse and drain the beans.
2. In a large, heavy pan, cook the beans until you judge that they are about half done. Drain the beans and discard the cooking water.
3. Return the beans to the pan and add the coconut milk, tomatoes, garlic, turmeric, and salt. Bring to a low boil, then reduce heat and simmer until the beans are tender.
4. Serve over rice.

IF YOU GO TO TANZANIA

The vast plains of the Serengeti host one of the earth's largest migrations. Countless wildebeest make the trek in a quest for survival as they seek fresh grass. You would expect to see wild animals on reserves or migration routes, but you might not be expecting the pink flamingos that live at the lakes. Tanzania is home to one of Africa's most diverse populations, but rivalry between tribes is almost nonexistent. Each tribe takes pride in its distinctive ceremonial clothing with intricate beadwork and accessories. If you visit Zanzibar, watch for intricately carved doors with brass ornamentation.

Coconut-Mushroom Soup

Lemongrass, with its distinctly Thai flavor, is sometimes difficult to find. If you are unable to find it in the produce section of your grocery store, simply make this lovely soup without it. With the exotic taste of coconut milk and fresh ginger, you might not miss it. *This recipe was inspired by my friend Judy Balkins.*

INGREDIENTS SERVES 4–6

1	14-oz. can coconut milk
2 c.	vegetable broth
6 pieces	fresh ginger, sliced into quarter-size coin slices
1 T.	lemongrass paste, or 1 stalk lemongrass (remove stalk before serving)
1	8-oz. pkg. extra-firm tofu, diced
1½ T.	oil
1 T.	soy sauce
2 c.	fresh white mushrooms, sliced
1 T.	fresh lime juice
1 t.	sugar
1 t.	Thai curry or chili paste

GARNISH

2 T. fresh basil leaves, cut into thin strips
3 T. fresh cilantro, chopped

PREPARATION

1. In a medium saucepan, combine the coconut milk, vegetable broth, ginger, and lemongrass paste. Bring to a boil over high heat.
2. In a separate pan, sauté the tofu in oil until lightly browned. Add the soy sauce, stirring quickly to coat the tofu. Add to the broth mixture.
3. Stir in the mushrooms, lime juice, sugar, and curry or chili paste.
4. Reduce heat and simmer for 5 to 10 minutes.
5. Garnish with fresh basil leaves and cilantro.

IF YOU GO TO THAILAND

A visit to Thailand would not be complete without visiting at least one of the thousands of Buddhist temples. To enter a temple, it is important to show proper respect. Your arms and legs must be covered, and you should take care not to step on a doorsill. The *wai* is the traditionally accepted greeting. Simply place your palms and fingers together at about chin level as if in prayer and nod your head once.

Potato-Barley Soup

This hearty soup is made with the simplest of ingredients. Barley, carrots, and potatoes are valuable staples that can grow in cold areas. They store well and are easy to keep on hand.

INGREDIENTS `SERVES 4–6`

2 T.	vegetable oil
1	large onion, diced
4 cloves	garlic, minced
8 c.	water or vegetable stock
½ c.	pearl barley
4	medium carrots, diced
5	medium potatoes, peeled and diced
1 t.	salt

PREPARATION

1. In a large pan, heat the oil and sauté the onion and garlic until translucent.
2. Add the water or vegetable stock, barley, and carrots. Bring to a boil; then reduce heat.
3. Simmer gently for 60 minutes.
4. Add the potatoes and salt. Simmer until potatoes are tender.
5. If the soup becomes too thick, add more water and heat through.

IF YOU GO TO TIBET

Tibet is often referred to as the "roof of the world," partly because it is home to Mount Everest. In this high, cold country, Tibetan life revolves around the yak. People are warmed by yak-dung fires and yak-butter lamps. Yak yogurt and cheese are part of their daily diet. The wool is used to weave clothing, blankets, and shelter. If you present a gift to someone, bend forward and hold the gift higher than your head with both hands. When you visit a monastery, it is expected that you walk through it clockwise. Do not touch religious artifacts or sit on religious objects. Tibetans are friendly people who will appreciate your efforts to be respectful of their cultural and religious traditions.

Black-Eyed Pea and Bell Pepper Soup

With black-eyed peas and bell peppers, this soup vibrates with Caribbean flavor. If you aren't afraid of fiery peppers, you might try adding a piece of Scotch bonnet pepper. If you do, take extra care not to use any of the seeds, and don't rub your eyes! Or you can play it safe and use a couple of jalapeño peppers, or add a dash of cayenne pepper. If you are feeling very cautious, simply enjoy the full flavors of all the other ingredients.

INGREDIENTS SERVES 4–6

1 T.	oil
1	medium green bell pepper, diced
1	medium red bell pepper, diced
1	medium yellow bell pepper, diced
2	medium onions, chopped
¼ c.	cilantro, chopped
3 c.	cooked black-eyed peas
4 c.	vegetable stock
2 c.	water
⅓ c.	brown rice
½ t.	ginger
½ t.	allspice
½ t.	thyme
½ t.	mustard power (mix with 1 T. of hot water)
1 t.	salt
1	medium fresh lime or lemon, cut into wedges

PREPARATION

1. Heat the oil in a large pan and add the bell peppers and onions. Stir over medium-high heat for 4 minutes or until the onions are slightly browned.
2. Stir in the cilantro, black-eyed peas, stock, water, rice, and spices except for the salt. Bring to a boil.
3. Cover and reduce heat to low. Simmer gently for 45 minutes. Add the salt.
4. Serve with lime or lemon wedges.

IF YOU GO TO TRINIDAD AND TOBAGO

These islands offer surfing, beachcombing, and hiking. Go snorkeling or take a ride on a glass-bottom boat to view the brilliantly colored tropical fish and the unique coral gardens. Spend some of your leisure time by renting a bicycle for a ride past waterfalls. You are bound to experience the vibrant calypso music during your stay, so if it pleases you, pick up a CD as a souvenir.

TUNISIA

Peanut-Tomato Soup

Adding peanut butter to soup might seem a little offbeat to some, but it is an essential ingredient to cuisine in nearly every African region. The winning combination of tomatoes, peanut butter, and rice makes this hearty soup well worth the effort.

INGREDIENTS SERVES 6–8

2 T.	olive oil
2	medium onions, chopped
1	large red bell pepper, chopped
4 cloves	garlic, chopped
3½ c.	canned crushed tomatoes with juice
8 c.	vegetable stock
¼ t.	chili powder
½ t.	salt
¾ c.	brown rice, uncooked
1 c.	crunchy peanut butter

PREPARATION

1. Heat the oil in a large stockpot over medium-high heat. Cook the onions and red pepper until lightly browned and tender. Add the garlic when the onion mixture is almost done.

2. Stir in the tomatoes, stock, chili powder, and salt. Reduce heat to low and simmer for 30 minutes.

3. Stir in the rice, cover, and simmer another 15 minutes or until the rice is tender. Stir in the peanut butter until blended well.

IF YOU GO TO TUNISIA

Tunisia has been a favorite vacation spot for Europeans who long to escape the cold and rain for sun-drenched beaches. While enjoying sunny, warm weather, you can visit cliffs with panoramic views of the Mediterranean Sea, coastal towns, or quaint inland villages. Tunisia is a good place to haggle for carpets to send back home. It also offers a vast selection of handcrafted mosaic art. Tunisia's Cape Blanc is the northernmost tip of the continent of Africa.

Cucumber Salad Soup

A traditional Turkish meal consists of several courses of elaborately prepared dishes. This refreshing soup is usually served ice cold in very small chilled bowls or teacups as an appetizer. For a more substantial soup, serve it in larger chilled bowls, pouring it over salad vegetables.

INGREDIENTS SERVES 4–6

1	large cucumber, peeled and chopped
1 clove	garlic, minced
1 T.	fresh lemon juice
2 c.	plain yogurt
2 T.	water
3 T.	olive oil
2 T.	fresh dill, chopped
2 t.	fresh mint, chopped

ADDITIONAL INGREDIENTS, OPTIONAL

This ice-cold cucumber soup is delicious poured over additional salad vegetables

- Cumbers, sliced thin
- Tomatoes, diced
- Carrots, grated
- Red or green bell pepper, chopped
- Artichoke hearts

PREPARATION

1. In a blender, puree the cucumber, garlic, and lemon juice, pulsing to liquefy.
2. Add the yogurt, water, oil, dill, and mint. Blend on high for 1 minute or until smooth.
3. Refrigerate until ice cold. Serve in small chilled cups, or pour over additional vegetables in chilled bowls.

IF YOU GO TO TURKEY

One of Istanbul's premier landmarks is the Blue Mosque. Visitors are welcome, although it is closed to nonworshipers for brief periods during prayer times. Show respect by stepping in with your right foot first. The Spice Market is one of the most famous in the world. For centuries, traders traveling on the Silk Road converged at this bustling hub to do business. Today, Turkey is described as a vacation destination where tourists come to enjoy the sun, sea, shopping, and colorful culture.

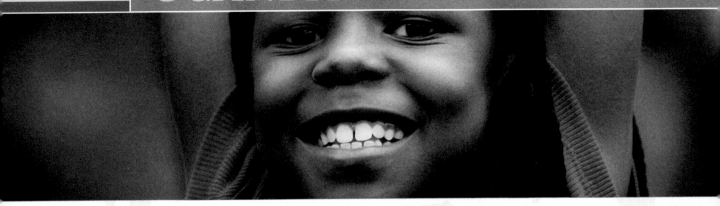

Savory Sweet Pea Soup

Check out the list of spices in this soup! You can turn up the heat by adding more cayenne pepper, or you can leave it out and enjoy the rest of the flavors.

INGREDIENTS SERVES 6–8

2 T.	vegetable oil
2	medium onions, chopped
3 cloves	garlic, minced
1 t.	fresh peeled ginger, grated
1 t.	salt
¼ t.	cayenne pepper, optional
1 t.	coriander
½ t.	cumin
¼ t.	cardamom
⅛ t.	ground cloves
¼ t.	cinnamon
½ t.	turmeric
2	medium tomatoes, chopped
1	medium sweet potato, chopped
3½ c.	water, divided
4 c.	frozen green peas

PREPARATION

1. Heat the oil. Sauté the onions and garlic for 5 to 10 minutes, or until tender.
2. Mix in the ginger, salt, and all the spices. Cook for a few minutes, stirring often. Do not let the mixture burn.
3. Add the tomatoes, sweet potato, and 1½ c. of water. Bring to a boil. Reduce heat, cover, and simmer for 10 minutes.
4. Add 2 c. of the peas and simmer for 10 minutes, or until sweet potato is tender.
5. Remove from heat and add remaining 2 c. of water.
6. Puree in batches in a blender until smooth.
7. Return to the pan and add the last 2 c. of peas. Cook over medium heat for 3 to 5 minutes until heated through.

IF YOU GO TO UGANDA

About half of the world's mountain gorillas reside in Uganda. Its lush forests provide a natural habitat to hundreds of species of birds and mammals. Winston Churchill, one of Uganda's earliest tourists, described the country as the "pearl of Africa," a moniker that is proudly used to this day. Ugandans have been described as an eloquent, open, and gracious people.

Ruby Borscht

Borscht is a thick, slow-cooked soup popular in the Ukraine, Russia, and parts of Central Asia. Its ingredients vary from country to country, but an essential ingredient is a deep red vegetable, such as beets, tomatoes, or even rhubarb. The end result is a nutritious jewel-colored soup.

INGREDIENTS SERVES 6–8

6 c.	water or vegetable stock
2	medium onions, sliced thin
2 cloves	garlic, minced
3	large fresh beets (about 1½ lb.), peeled and diced into 1-inch cubes
1	medium cabbage (white, green, or red), shredded
2	carrots, sliced in rounds
2	stalks celery, sliced
1	large potato, peeled and diced into ½ inch cubes
1 c.	tomato juice
1 t.	sugar
3 T.	fresh dill, chopped
2 T.	fresh lemon or lime juice

GARNISH, OPTIONAL

1 c. sour cream
2 T. fresh dill, chopped

PREPARATION

1. In a large pot, add the water or vegetable stock, onions, garlic, and beets. Bring to a boil over medium heat. Cover and cook for 20 minutes.
2. Add the remaining ingredients except for the dill and lemon or lime juice. Cover and simmer over low heat for 40 minutes, or until vegetables are tender.
3. Add the dill and lemon or lime juice and stir well.
4. Garnish if desired, and serve.

IF YOU GO TO THE UKRAINE

Grandparents are much-valued members in Ukrainian families and are very involved in caring for their grandchildren. Elderly women are sometimes affectionately referred to as security guards because they observe everything and miss nothing. If the weather cooperates, they spend much of the day sitting outside and visiting with passersby. Even when the weather is bad, they keep watch from a window and manage to keep up with everything that is happening. Ukrainian stitch work is known for its intricate designs. The detailed handiwork is often replicated in stoneware or decorative arts.

Butter Bean–Carrot Soup

Butter beans, similar to broad beans or large lima beans, are not used as often as other legumes, but they are incredibly tasty. Shake up your usual menus and give butter beans a try. Either cook the dry beans, or use the canned variety as a convenient shortcut.

INGREDIENTS SERVES 6–8

1 T.	olive oil
1	large onion, chopped
3 cloves	garlic, minced
1	medium hot pepper, chopped fine
2 c.	tomatoes, chopped (fresh or canned, with juice)
8 c.	water
6 c.	cooked butter beans, drained
3	medium carrots, chopped fine
1	medium potato, peeled and diced into ½-inch cubes
½ c.	cilantro, chopped fine
1½ t.	salt
¾ t.	cumin

PREPARATION

1. In a large pan, heat the oil and sauté the onion, garlic, and hot pepper for 10 minutes.

2. Add the remaining ingredients and bring to a boil. Cover, reduce heat, and simmer for 20 to 30 minutes, or until vegetables are tender.

3. Add more water if the soup is too thick.

IF YOU GO TO THE UNITED ARAB EMIRATES

The United Arab Emirates, comprised of seven emirates, borders the Gulf of Oman and the Persian Gulf. A visit to Dubai would definitely include shopping. You can find everything from high-end designer labels at glitzy malls to super bargains at street markets. Take a look at the ultramodern skyscrapers for which the city has become famous. If you're up for an adventure, join a desert safari to see the vast sand dunes in the Margham Desert, including the Big Red Dunes, famous for their distinctive color. If you're touring the desert on a Friday, you might get to watch camel races.

Mushroom and Wild Rice Soup

Wild rice is native to North America and grows predominantly in the Great Lakes region. It is not actually rice but the seed of a water grass that thrives in cold shallow water, especially in Minnesota and Wisconsin. Native Americans initially harvested the grains by shaking the seeds into a canoe, but now it is more likely that a flotation combine does the job.

INGREDIENTS SERVES 4

3 c.	vegetable broth
⅓ c.	wild rice
1	medium onion, diced
1 T.	oil
1 c.	nonfat, regular half-and-half, or evaporated milk
2 T.	flour
1 t.	fresh thyme
2 c.	fresh white mushrooms, sliced
	salt to taste

PREPARATION

1. In a medium pan, combine the vegetable broth and uncooked wild rice. Bring to a boil; then reduce heat and simmer, covered, for 40 minutes.
2. In a separate pan, heat the oil and sauté the onion.
3. Combine the half-and-half or evaporated milk, flour, and thyme.
4. Stir into the rice mixture and add the mushrooms and sautéed onions.
5. Stir until thick and bubbly.

IF YOU GO TO THE UNITED STATES

Americans tend to be rather informal and are quick to address one another by their first names. They also appreciate courtesy and fair play, such as when joining a line. It is expected that you will join at the end of the line rather than jumping ahead of others. Most Americans are proud of their work ethic, but they greatly value leisure time for recreation and family activities. Many are loyal fans of college and university sports. National parks, such as Yellowstone, the Grand Canyon, Yosemite, Acadia, and the Great Smoky Mountains, are considered natural treasures. The parks receive millions of visitors each year.

UZBEKISTAN

Fragrant Pomegranate–Lentil Soup

Pomegranate juice, herbs, and spices bring astonishing results when simmered with lentils and spinach. The result is a fragrance and taste that is slightly floral. This special recipe has probably been adapted many times over the centuries, but it is still new if you've never tried it.

INGREDIENTS SERVES 6–8

3 T.	vegetable oil
2 t.	cumin seeds
2	large onions, thinly sliced
3 cloves	garlic, minced
1/3 c.	yellow split peas
1/2 c.	lentils
4 c.	water
4 c.	pomegranate juice
1/4 t.	cinnamon
1 T.	sugar
1 lb.	baby spinach
1/2 c.	rice
3/4 c.	fresh dill, chopped
3/4 c.	fresh parsley, chopped
3/4 c.	fresh mint, chopped
	salt to taste

GARNISH

1 c. fresh pomegranate seeds

PREPARATION

1. Heat the oil in a large, heavy pot over medium heat. Add the cumin seeds and stir-fry for 20 seconds until aromatic.
2. Add the onions and garlic and stir-fry for 10 minutes.
3. Add the split peas and lentils, stirring for 3 minutes.
4. Add the water and bring to a boil. Reduce heat and simmer for 20 minutes.
5. Stir in the pomegranate juice, cinnamon, sugar, spinach, rice, dill, parsley, and mint. Bring back to a boil, then reduce heat and simmer for 30 minutes. Add salt to taste.
6. Ladle into bowls. Garnish with pomegranate seeds.

IF YOU GO TO UZBEKISTAN

In Uzbekistan special tea rituals are still practiced. The tea is poured from a ceramic pot into the host's teacup, and then poured back into the teapot. This is repeated three times. Next, each teacup will be filled half full. This allows the steaming tea to cool rapidly so that guests may quench their thirst.

Asparagus Soup

Smooth and luxurious, this special soup is fabulous either hot or cold. If you are having guests and want to save time, it can be made a day before. It could also work as an appetizer or chilled course for a fine dinner. Asparagus is used in traditional recipes around Christmas time in Venezuela.

INGREDIENTS `SERVES 4–6`

3½ to 4 c.	asparagus, cut into short pieces
3 c.	vegetable stock or water
¼ c.	margarine
2	medium onions, chopped
4 T.	all-purpose flour
¼ t.	coriander
½ t.	salt
1 t.	fresh lemon juice
2 c.	milk
½ c.	cream (may substitute yogurt or buttermilk)

PREPARATION

1. Wash and trim the asparagus, discarding the woody ends. Use a vegetable peeler to trim off any rough knobs. Fine asparagus does not need to be trimmed.
2. Place the asparagus in a pan with the vegetable stock or water and bring to a boil. Cover and simmer for about 20 minutes, or until very tender. Strain the asparagus, but keep the stock or cooking water and set aside.
3. In a medium pan, melt the margarine and sauté the onions over low heat. Do not let them get brown. Stir in the flour quickly to coat the onions. Cook for 1 minute.
4. Gradually add the reserved vegetable stock or cooking water, whisking until smooth. Bring back to a boil. Simmer for 3 minutes until thickened.
5. Add the asparagus, coriander, salt, and lemon juice. Simmer for 10 minutes.
6. Remove from heat. Transfer to a blender and process until smooth. Return to a clean pan (or rinse the one you were using) and add the milk. Bring to a low boil and simmer for 2 minutes.
7. Stir in the cream, reheat gently, and serve.

IF YOU GO TO VENEZUELA

Unlike sports fans in other countries of South America, Venezuelans tend to prefer baseball over football. All kinds of adventure sports, including wild water rafting and paragliding, are available to those who love the outdoors. The tallest waterfall in the world is Angel Falls in the Parque Nacional Canaima, dropping close to 1,000 meters, or about 300 stories.

VIETNAM

Curried Mushroom-Carrot Soup

This spicy soup looks beautiful when served in Asian bowls. The bean sprouts and cilantro add a bit of crunch and color to the top of each serving. *This recipe is in honor of my friend Truoc Huynh.*

INGREDIENTS · SERVES 4–6

2 T.	oil
4	green onions, chopped
2 cloves	garlic, chopped
1 T.	fresh ginger, peeled and grated
3 T.	curry powder
1	medium green bell pepper, chopped
2	medium carrots, thinly sliced on the diagonal
8 to 10	white mushrooms, sliced
1 lb.	fried tofu
4 c.	vegetable broth
3 c.	water
¼ t.	red pepper flakes (according to taste)
1 or 2	bay leaves
2 c.	diced potatoes
1¾ c.	coconut milk

GARNISH

2 c. fresh bean sprouts, chopped
¼ c. cilantro, chopped

PREPARATION

1. Heat the oil in a large stockpot over medium heat; sauté the onions until translucent. Stir in the garlic, ginger, and curry powder. Cook for about 4 minutes.
2. Stir in the green pepper, carrots, mushrooms, and tofu. Add the vegetable broth and water and bring to a boil.
3. Add the red pepper flakes, bay leaves, potatoes, and coconut milk. When the soup returns to a boil, reduce heat and simmer for 40 to 50 minutes, or until the potatoes are tender.
4. Top each serving with a pile of bean sprouts and cilantro.

IF YOU GO TO VIETNAM

Natural beauty abounds in this long, narrow country. If you get up before dawn in Hanoi and hurry down to the Hoan Kiem Lake, you can join other folks who start exercising together at 5:00 A.M. Vietnam is known for tailors who do excellent work at good prices. Take a trip through the countryside to admire the rice paddies, or take a boat ride on the Mekong River. Make a point of chatting with the friendly Vietnamese people, and take photos to remember them by.

Leek and Potato Soup

The leek is widely recognized as the national symbol of Wales, but the true origins of this icon are unclear. Some say that soldiers were ordered to wear the leek on their helmets before battle. Others say it refers to a battle that took place in a field full of leeks. Does it really matter? Not while you savor this comforting, country-style soup.

INGREDIENTS SERVES 4–6

1½ T.	margarine
3	medium leeks, white part only, sliced lengthwise and chopped
3	large potatoes, peeled and diced
½ t.	salt
4 c.	boiling water
1 c.	evaporated milk

PREPARATION

1. In a large, heavy pan, melt the margarine and sauté the leeks, stirring frequently for about 10 minutes.
2. Add the diced potatoes and salt, stirring over medium-high heat for 2 minutes.
3. Pour the boiling water over the potatoes and cover. Simmer for about 20 minutes over low heat, stirring occasionally.
4. When the potatoes are soft, drain about half of the water. Use a potato masher to break down the vegetables, but it doesn't need to be smooth. (If you prefer a chunkier texture, don't bother to mash the potatoes.)
5. Add the evaporated milk and reheat until the soup simmers.

IF YOU GO TO WALES

The beautiful custom of giving lovespoons as a token of affection began in Wales in the fifteenth century and continues today. Traditional lovespoons are carved from a single piece of wood with elaborate designs in the handle and sometimes in the bowl of the spoon. With symbolic expressions laden with personal meaning, a suitor would give it to a young lady to celebrate a marriage proposal. Over time, lovespoons have been given to commemorate other important occasions such as Mother's Day, graduations, or birthdays.

Sweet Potato–Date Soup

You'll taste a little sweetness in this vegetable soup, but it has a very subtle flavor. It's an unusual way to use dates, but it works very well with the sweet potatoes. Fine dining, served from your own kitchen.

INGREDIENTS SERVES 4–6

2 T.	oil
1	medium onion, chopped
3	large sweet potatoes or yams, peeled and chopped or diced
½ c.	fresh or dried pitted dates, chopped
4 c.	vegetable stock
1 c.	water
½ t.	salt

GARNISH

⅓ c. chopped walnuts, optional

PREPARATION

1. Heat the oil and sauté the onion until tender.
2. Add the sweet potatoes or yams and cook over low heat for 7 minutes, stirring frequently.
3. Add the dates, vegetable stock, water, and salt. Bring to a boil; then reduce heat and simmer for 15 minutes or until the sweet potatoes or yams are tender.
4. Puree the mixture in a blender until smooth. Return to the pan and reheat.
5. Serve hot. Top with chopped walnuts if desired.

IF YOU GO TO WESTERN SAHARA

To conduct a council meeting without tea would be inconceivable. Any kind of gathering in Western Sahara is an appropriate occasion to serve tea. There are at least three long-held traditions that are keenly observed: (1) tea is best enjoyed in the company of others; (2) the longer the process of making tea, the more time you have to talk; and (3) the best tea is prepared over a fire. One of the most prized possessions anyone can have is a camel. The relationship between camel and owner is often described as a very devoted one. Camels tend to be calm and efficient, even in extreme climates, and are known for their faithfulness.

Lentil and Green Pea Stew

This is one of those wonderful, expandable recipes. If unexpected visitors arrive, just add a bit more water, tomatoes, or other vegetables. Adjust the seasoning as needed, and no one will guess you had to make last-minute changes.

INGREDIENTS SERVES 6–8

5 c.	water
2 c.	lentils
2 T.	margarine
1	large onion, diced
2 cloves	garlic, minced
1 t.	cumin
1 T.	Hungarian sweet paprika
2 c.	tomatoes, fresh or canned, chopped fine
1 c.	tomato sauce
½ c.	tomato paste
1½ c.	frozen green peas, thawed
1½ t.	salt

PREPARATION

1. Bring the water to a boil and add the lentils. Reduce heat and simmer for 30 minutes, or until the lentils are tender. Add more water if necessary.
2. In a separate pan, melt the margarine and sauté the onion and garlic until the onion is translucent. Add the onion, garlic, cumin, and paprika, stirring to prevent burning.
3. Stir the onion and spices into the lentils. Add the tomatoes, tomato sauce, and tomato paste to the lentils, stirring to combine. Bring back to a simmer.
4. Add the green peas and salt. Cook for 5 minutes.
5. Serve over couscous or with pita bread, if desired.

IF YOU GO TO YEMEN

It is important for both men and women to dress modestly while in Yemen. Foreign women are not expected to cover their heads or wear a veil, but arms and legs should be covered. Keep necklines high and wear loose clothing. By respecting the local culture, you will have more opportunities to interact with people while you are there. Folks usually eat three times a day at home. Breakfast starts early with strong tea, the main meal is served hot in a stone or clay bowl, and a light supper might consist of vegetables and a side dish of dates. Very old homes that were built with partitioned areas for men and women may also have separate staircases. Furniture is often kept at a minimum, but cushions and mattresses are kept along the wall for seating. The floors are likely covered with goat-hair rugs.

Sweet Potato–Turnip Stew

This chunky stew is a great addition to your stew repertoire. You can substitute rutabagas for the turnips if you wish. Enjoy this as a stew, or serve it over rice or couscous.

INGREDIENTS SERVES 6–8

2 T.	oil
2	large onions, chopped
8 c.	water
1 t.	salt
½ c.	tomato paste
1¼ c.	peanut butter
2 c.	tomatoes, fresh or canned, diced
4	medium sweet potatoes or yams, peeled and diced
8	medium carrots, sliced
6	medium turnips, peeled and diced
1	small cabbage, chopped
10 to 12	okra, cut into ½-inch pieces
1	medium chili pepper, or ½ t. cayenne pepper

PREPARATION

1. In a large, heavy pan, cook the onions in oil until they begin to turn light brown.

2. Add the water and salt and bring to a boil.
3. In a separate bowl, add 1 c. of the boiling water to the tomato paste and peanut butter to make a thin paste. Stir it into the pan of boiling water and whisk until smooth.
4. Add the tomatoes, sweet potatoes, carrots, and turnips and bring back to a boil. Cover and cook for 15 minutes.
5. Stir in the cabbage and okra, reduce heat, and simmer for 20 minutes or until all the vegetables are tender. Add the chili pepper or ½ t. of cayenne pepper during the last 10 minutes of cooking

IF YOU GO TO ZAMBIA

The easygoing people of Zambia are known for their warm welcome to visitors. They have much to be proud of in their country. It has been said that the best-trained safari guides are in Zambia, ready to show you the best possible views of wildlife in national parks. You can take taxi boats across lakes, catch a view of Victoria Falls from the Zambian side, and meet tribal folks and learn about their traditions. A warm smile will pave the way to opportunities for interesting conversations.

Peanut Butter–Spinach Stew

If you are looking for something different to serve over rice, couscous, or cornmeal, give this stew a try. It is especially nice in the summer when you want a warm meal without heating up the kitchen with your oven.

INGREDIENTS SERVES 4–6

2 T.	margarine
2	large onions, chopped fine
3 cloves	garlic, minced
1 t.	salt
1	medium chili pepper or ½ t. cayenne pepper
2 c.	water
2	medium green bell peppers, chopped
3 c.	tomatoes, fresh or canned, diced
1 lb.	fresh spinach (may substitute kale or other greens)
⅓ c.	smooth peanut butter

PREPARATION

1. In a large pan, melt the margarine and sauté the onions until golden brown. Add the garlic, salt, and chili pepper or cayenne pepper. Cook for 2 minutes.
2. Add the water, green bell peppers, and tomatoes. Bring to a boil, then reduce heat and simmer for 5 to 10 minutes until the bell peppers are tender.
3. Meanwhile, in a separate large pan, bring additional water to boil. Cook the spinach until leaves have wilted and stems are tender. Drain the spinach.
4. Place the peanut butter in a small bowl. Take ¼ c. of hot broth from the bell peppers and tomatoes and stir it into the peanut butter to make a paste. Add the peanut butter paste to the tomato mixture.
5. Add the drained spinach to the stew and simmer gently until heated through. Adjust liquid if needed.
6. Serve over rice or couscous.

IF YOU GO TO ZIMBABWE

The powerful, thundering Victoria Falls has been called one of the seven natural wonders of the world. It has also been referred to as the "greatest known curtain of falling water" by early explorers. This country is also home to a large number of rhinoceros. River safaris are available for those who like adventure. Those who like shopping will have no trouble finding meticulously made handicrafts and woodcarvings.